Endorsements

"This book is the all-inclusive cookbook for the recipe of personal responsibility and emergency preparedness. It contains pages of ideas and implantable solutions that will save lives and anguish. I've trained, lived and taught emergency preparedness for the last thirty-eight years and I learned from this book! *Get Your Stuff Together* is over 200 pages of common sense that will bring calm to the storm of life. Job well done."
        Michael F. Staley, Public Health Advisor, Centers for Disease Control and Prevention

"If you only read one book this year or in a lifetime read this one. This book will profoundly change the way you protect yourself and your family.
        Mark V. Cerney, President/Founder Next of Kin Registry (NOKR)

"With the unusual number of disasters in the US and around the world the last few years, this book should be in every home in America. The worst part about the loss so many families have experienced, is that so much of it could have been so easily prevented, with the simple steps found throughout *Get Your Stuff Together*."
        Sara Feigenholtz, State Representative, Illinois General Assembly

"*Get Your Stuff Together* is an amazing volume that provides a clear roadmap for gathering and organizing vital information. The book offers logical and specific resources about how to prepare for or cope with emergencies - including step-by-step instructions and comprehensive forms that consider every detail. The book is a lifesaver for avoiding or coping with disasters big or small."
        Christine Zrinsky, Vice President for Development, Lincoln Park Zoo

"Impacted by a personal family tragedy, Laura & Janet Greenwald set off to take a stand for families and make a negative circumstance into a very positive one, many times over. Buy *Get Your Stuff Together* for your family or as a gift for your loved ones. It just takes one afternoon to get you and your family fully prepared. Buying this book and taking simple action now can seriously save lives, heartache down the road and keep you from saying, "Oh, if only we had taken the time to get the family prepared."
        Brian Ouellette, President & Founder Pro Athlete Direct and Shoewallet Active Gear

"*Get Your Stuff Together* is an amazing wealth of information, and a "must have", "must follow" book. The direct way that Janet and Laura present the material makes it easy to grasp the value of the topic. But what's really great is the way they've folded in real life stories which bring all the guidance down to me personally. I also love the stories about companies I'm familiar with and how they approach Emergency Management."
        Ric Skinner, Owner/Consultant at The Stoneybrook Group

"Exceptional! The Greenwalds took their outstanding book *Ready In 10* and put it on steroids! You hear "plan". But for what? Why? How? What are the critical pieces of information I should have? This book is for you, and about you -- saving, recovering, even thriving when misfortunes, from small to catastrophic, come your way. Not sure "how to"? See their recommended "Cool Tools" section."

Clint Steele, PhD -- USGS Emeritus Geologist, CERT Trainer

GET YOUR STUFF TOGETHER

How to Keep from Losing the Things
That Make Your Life, *Your Life*

Written By

JANET GREENWALD
&
LAURA GREENWALD

Published by Stuf Productions

LION AND THE ROCK
ENTERTAINMENT

Copyright © 2014, 2017 Lion and the Rock Entertainment

All rights reserved, including the right to reproduce this book or portions thereof in any form whatsoever.

"Get Your Stuff Together," "GET YOUR STUFF TOGETHER" and the forms and plans within, should be used for general information purposes only. Readers using the information herein, agree to hold NOKEP, Stuf Productions, Lion And The Rock Entertainment and the authors, harmless from any liability incurred by its use. All information contained within is copyrighted and may not be republished without written permission.

For information about special discounts and bulk purchases go to www.getyourstufftogether.com or email webmaster1@nokep.org.

Manufactured in the United States of America

ISBN: 978-1475027457

Table Of Contents

Before You Begin — 6

Your Things

Home Inventory	13
Data	16
Print Photos	19
Digital Photos	23
Home Videos/Home Movies	27
Music	30
Family Recipes	34
Family History	37
Voice Mails or Special Recordings That You Want to Keep	41
How to Make Your Breakable Keepsakes More Disaster Resistant	44
How to Keep From Losing or Destroying Your Cell Phone	46

Yourself & Your Family

Vital Documents	51
Contacts and Address Books	54
Facebook & LinkedIn Contacts	58
Your Business	62
Social Media Accounts	64
Bank Accounts and Money	65
Financial Information	68
Insurance	71

Your Life

It's All About Communication	77
Medical Information	79
How To Put An ICE Contact On Your Phone	82
How To Fill Out Your Family's Emergency Contact Cards	86
Emergency Wallet Cards	89
Family Evacuation Plan	91
Evacuation Checklist	96
Get Back To Life Plan	99
How To Make Your Family Findable	102
Mobile Command Center	106

Secrets From The Experts — 113

GYST Forms & Emergency Action Plans — 167

FOREWORD

I met Laura and Janet Greenwald nearly a decade ago as our paths crossed in the Next of Kin/Emergency Contact field. Their efforts included new legislation with U.S. Representative Jesse Jackson, Jr. and a highly successfully national campaign to educate hospitals and Americans on the importance of Next of Kin Notification. Their passion and steam was sadly born out of personal loss and frustration with the system. But this dynamic team has taken this personal tragedy and expanded on it to help and educate all of us.

In America like many other countries, we battle the complacency factor, living as if we will never need to prepare for emergencies. I've seen my share of overnight visionaries, many born out of the various global and daily disasters I deal with. These efforts though commendable sadly lose the momentum and fail to last or impress me or the world we live in. I've truly only met one team who has battled through and will change the way we get prepared, and that is the Greenwalds.

If you only read one book this year or in a lifetime read this one. This book will profoundly change the way you protect yourself and your family. Life does not give many second chances or a rewind button, so trust in the expertise of Janet and Laura Greenwald.

Mark V. Cerney
President/Founder Next of Kin Registry (NOKR)

Before You Begin

Before You Begin

Before we get started, go ahead and download GET YOUR STUFF TOGETHER Forms and Action Plans along with the other bonus material you received with this book. There's some awesome stuff in there, so be sure to look through it! Just go to www.getyourstufftogether.com/backupplandwld.htm and register with the special code tbp2015 to confirm that you're a book owner.

Set Up A New Folder On Your Computer

As you go through this book, you're going to be backing up all of your photos, music, home videos, keepsakes and other information, so you'll need a place to put it, right? Create a folder on your computer desktop and name it "Backup Data (dd/mm/yy)".

Now create two new folders within that folder. For the first one, name it something easy to remember like "GET YOUR STUFF TOGETHER Forms".

Open up GET YOUR STUFF TOGETHER Forms and Action Plans zip file that you just downloaded and copy and paste the files within it, into that new folder for safekeeping.

The second folder we want you to create, will hold all of your family's Forms and Plans. Name this something like "Our Family's Forms and Action Plans".

Then every time you complete a form, save it inside the folder. That way you'll know where everything is when it comes time to copy and store them for safekeeping.

For an extra measure of safety and convenience, you can also print out all of the forms when completed, place them in a three ring binder and then toss the binder into your Plastic Evacuation Bin, where it will be ready and waiting the next time you need them.

If You Won't Be Using A Computer

You'll also find all of the forms and plans in the back of this book. You can fill them out right in the book and then toss the book into your Backup Plan Evacuation Bin, where it will be ready and waiting the next time you need it.

How To Use The Downloadable Forms and Action Plans

All of the forms in the zip file are meant to be used over and over again. That means that when you're ready to use a form, you should immediately SAVE IT WITH A NEW NAME, like John Jones Medical or Smith Family Home Inventory. Otherwise, you'll overwrite the original document, which kind of defeats the purpose.

And this way you will always have the original file, so you can have a new clean copy to work from, or let another person in your family use it. Once you complete your forms and plans you'll also be able to change them and reprint them any time you need to update your information.

When you open the Forms and Plans in Microsoft Word, you'll notice that each of them has places for you to enter your information:

Bank	Account Number	Branch
My Favorite Bank FDIC		
Website	User Name/PIN	Customer Service
Myfavoritebank.com		

They work just like any other document in Word. Simply move your mouse/cursor, click inside one of the empty boxes, and then begin typing your information into the empty box (as we've done with My Favorite Bank FDIC above).

If you don't have enough room for your information, all you have to do is make the box longer. To do this, move your mouse over the bottom line of the box you want to lengthen. As you hover over it, it will turn into an arrow. Click and pull the line down, to adjust the length of the box. It will turn into a dotted line as in the picture below and you can pull it down until you're satisfied with the length. Just release the mouse button and type in the rest of your information.

places for you to enter your information:

Bank	Account Number	Branch	Checking/Savings?
Trust Bank & Loan			
Website	User Name/PIN	Customer Service	Notes

And if you want to add extra lines to the form (let's say you have four bank accounts instead of three), either insert extra rows where you want them, or if you're at the end of a section, place your cursor in the last box on the line and hit the Tab Button to create as many new lines as you need.

Where To Store The Forms, Action Plans and Data You Placed In Your Backup Folder

Of course you'll keep a copy of your Backup Plan Forms and Action Plans right in the house with you, but what if a disaster or emergency occurs when you're away from home or are unable to access your computer? We've got you covered. Once you've completed the Forms and Plans, you can save them and store them in at least three secure locations.

If your forms, action plans, and vital documents are **on your computer, you can place them on a password-protected flash drive or portable hard drive:**
- And take them with you during evacuation in your evacuation bin or on a key ring.
- And place it in a safe deposit box or water/fireproof safe in your own city.
- And place it in a safe deposit box, water/fireproof safe, or with relatives in the city where you'll be evacuating.
- Or place the forms and documents in a password-protected online file repository or the file directory of your family's personal web site. This way if you need a copy of your information or forms quickly, you can retrieve them from any Internet-enabled computer, cellphone or tablet.

If your forms, action plans, and vital documents are **on paper, you can place them:**
- In a safe deposit box or water/fireproof safe in your own city.
- In your Plastic Evacuation Bin. Only place the documents that you actually need in this bin. Remember that evacuating during hurricanes or tornadoes can be hard on documents, so it's better to take scans with you or leave originals or copies in water resistant safe deposit boxes away from the affected area.
- In a safe deposit box, water/fireproof safe, or with relatives in the city where you'll be evacuating.

One important note: DO NOT put your or your family's social security numbers or sensitive financial information or in online folders or in the Cloud, no matter how secure you feel they are. If you have to have those numbers with you (and haven't memorized them), copy or scan the originals and place them in a secure safe deposit box instead.

How To Copy and Move Files On Your PC
- The simplest way to copy a large amount of files on a PC is to:
  - Highlight the files you wish to copy either by clicking on them while holding down the shift key or choosing them with your mouse.
  - Hold down the CTRL key + the letter C at the same time to copy them.
  - Open the Backup folder, click your mouse inside and hold down the CTRL key + the letter V to paste all of the files inside of the new folder.

How To Copy and Move Files On Your Mac

Hold down the Option Key (⌥ or **Alt**) and click on the file that you want to move, then drag it and drop it in its new location. Double check to make sure that there is a copy of the file in the old and the new locations.

How To Download a ZIP file

To download a zip file, right click on the link, choose "Save Target As", and save the Zip file to your desktop. If you would rather, you can also download and save each document one by one. For more information go to:
http://getyourstufftogether.com/download/downloadingdocuments.pdf

How To Open a ZIP File
A ZIP file is a little folder that holds all of your documents zipped up inside for easy downloading. Once you download it, you'll see a little icon that looks like a file box. Double click on it, it will open and all the files will appear.

You can extract the documents one of two ways: 1) Click the extract button and all of the files will be extracted from the box and land on your desktop. 2) Highlight all the files, click CTRL+C to copy them and then CTRL+V to paste them onto your desktop.

How to Get a Copy of Adobe's Free Adobe Reader PDF Software
Go to www.adobe.com and follow the instructions to download the latest free PDF software from their website.

Your Things

Home Inventory

Are you at home right now? If so, put the book down and close your eyes for a minute. Go around the room in your mind and try to picture each item. Focus especially on the items that mean a great deal to you or have a significant financial value. Everything that you would want to replace if that room were destroyed.

When you're certain you've remembered everything, open your eyes.

Now look around the room.

Did you remember everything you would want to replace?

Do you know off the top of your head what items were still under warranty, what was insured and for how much?

In other words, if this hadn't been an exercise, but had been an insurance agent or a police officer writing down a list of your valuables after a burglary or a hurricane, would you have been happy with the list you made?

I didn't think so. Memory is a wonderful thing, but it can be affected by many factors, like stress, trauma and fatigue – exactly the things that happen after an emergency. That's why putting together a list of your treasured or valued objects while they're still in front of you, is a MUCH better idea.

So grab your cameras – regular, video or one that shoots both – and let's get to it.

By the way if you have kids in the house, this is a great project for them. Once you decide which items to include, send them off with a list and a video or digital camera and have them take photos of each item. Either way, this task is easy to do.

Organized

How To Make Your Own Home Inventory List

Your Mission, Should You Choose To Accept It...

...is to create a list of all of the objects of value in your home. By the end of this Shortcut Sheet, you'll have a list of everything you would need to replace anything in your home that's expensive, insured, under warranty or simply of value to you. So open the Home Inventory Form (you'll find it inside the Backup Plan Forms you downloaded at the beginning of the book) and we'll get started.

1. You'll Need Your Camera & A Pencil

Go get your digital camera, a video camera if you have one, your Home Inventory List and a pencil. Once you're ready, begin walking through each room of your home, starting with your living room, usually home to the most expensive electronic equipment.

2. Document All The Info You Can Find

Write down the name of each valued item, along with a short description, the manufacturer, serial number and any other information you know about it.

If you have a copy of your warranty information or original purchase receipts for any of the valued items, note that information as well on the Home Inventory List, then put the documents aside until Step 5.

3. Document The Current Condition

As you stop at each item, take a digital photo of it to show its current condition. If the item is damaged in a disaster, you'll have proof of the item's original condition to give to the claims adjuster. It will also remind you what the item looked like, if it ever needs to be replaced

4. Spielberg Revisited

Once you're finished with the room, grab your video camera and do a quick video tour. Make sure to say which room it is and the current date.

First do a sweep of the room to show where everything is and the general condition of the room.

Then do a close-up of each of the valued items on your list. Show the front, back, sides and any model/serial numbers or identifying marks.

Paperwork, Paperwork 5

Gather all of the warranties, protection plans, certificates of insurance, provenance papers and receipts that you have for the items you listed, and put them together in the same location.

It doesn't matter whether it is a file folder or a section inside your safe. Just make sure that every time you purchase a new item, that you put all of the paperwork that comes with it, in that same location.

Now For Safekeeping... 6

Print, scan or make three copies of the Home Inventory List, the walking tour photos, the video and the warranties, receipts and other documents that you located earlier and store them in at least **three** secure, damage-proof locations.

That way if one or two of the locations are inaccessible, you'll still be able to grab the information you need and get it to your insurance agent. In fact, ask your agent if you can also leave a copy with him/her for safekeeping.

Data

Many people think that, because they have all of their documents, photos, videos, recipes, contacts and other data stored on their computer hard drive, those files are safe. And for the most part, they're right. Putting your files on a computer is safer than having them in a dusty old file cabinet. And on a computer, you can easily search for and find documents in seconds.

But, don't forget that a computer is very much like that file cabinet. It may not be vulnerable to moths and dust, but hard drives can stop working and documents can become corrupted or accidently deleted.

So what can you do?

Back up your files. Often. And by often, we mean at least once a month – once a week if you're always creating or editing new documents. Then make sure you save that data to more than one back up drive in more than one safe location. For instance use two portable hard drives and store one drive in a different room than your computer and the second at work or in a safe deposit box.

By the way, here's a quick tip that really saved us a lot of time and energy this past year. One day I downloaded the latest Microsoft update only to have it wreak havoc with our computer. A few days later it was only getting worse. So I grabbed our ClickFree backup drive – we have the CS6 Easy Imaging model and plugged it in to the PC. Why? The reason we bought it. It not only backs up and restores your computer files but it also backs up your ENTIRE system, software and all. One hour later, I had restored it to pre-meltdown condition and it's worked perfectly ever since. One drive, one button, zero headaches. Was it worth the $99? You bet!

So are you ready to back up your date? Then let's get started.

Organized

How To Back Up Your Data

Your Mission, Should You Choose To Accept It...

...is to back up and then archive all of your data, not only to keep it safe, but to be able to access it in alternate locations if your home or office is ever compromised or inaccessible. So let's get started!

First You Have To Find It — 1

Grab a pencil and paper and make a list of the data you currently have on your computer, removable disks or CDs, that you would need to access in an emergency, or that you absolutely cannot replace if lost or destroyed.

Here are a few ideas to get you started:
- Digital Photos
- Downloaded Music Files
- Videos
- Contacts
- Work/Vital Documents
- Financial Documents/Files
- Tax Documents/Files
- Presentations
- Books you've purchased or downloaded
- Articles or Papers that you have authored
- Anything else you or your family have created that you do not want to lose.

Here's How To Back It Up — 2

Using the list you just compiled, locate the data that you want to safeguard, on your computer.

Create a new folder on your computer desktop and name it "Backup Data (dd/mm/yy)," with today's date.

You're going to copy the files and place the copies in the Backup Folder and leave the original files where they are on your computer.

The simplest way to copy a large amount of files on a PC is to:
- Highlight the files you wish to copy either by clicking on them while holding down the shift key, or choosing them with your mouse.
- Hold down the CTRL key + the letter C at the same time to copy them.
- Then double click your Backup folder to open it. Click your mouse inside the folder and hold down the CTRL key + the letter V to paste all of the files inside the new folder.

The simplest way to copy a large amount of files on a Mac is to:
- Hold down the Option Key (⌥ or **Alt**) and click on the file that you want to move, then drag it and drop it in its new location.

After copying and pasting your folders into the Backup Folder, double check to make sure that there is a copy of the file in the old and the new location.

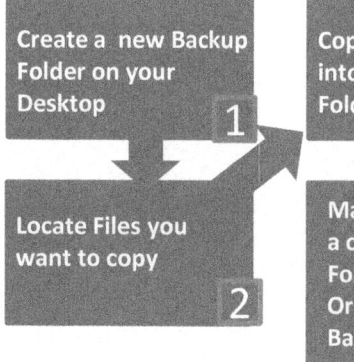

The Best Place To Put Your Data Is... 3

Where you need it to be and where it will be the safest. Where you decide to secure and store your information is up to you. But here are a few ideas:

- Place files on a **flash drive** or **portable hard drive**, that you can take with during evacuation on a **key ring or in your evacuation bin**.
- Place files on a **flash drive** or **portable hard drive**, that's located in a **safe deposit box** or **water/fireproof safe** in **your own city**.
- Place the **flash drive** or **portable hard drive**, that's located in a **safe deposit box**, **water/fireproof safe**, or with relatives in the **city where you'll be evacuating**.
- Place files on a files on a **password-protected online file repository**, in the Cloud or even the file directory of your family's personal web site. This way if you need a copy of your data quickly, you can retrieve it from any Internet-enabled computer.

Important! Please Remember... 4

DO NOT put your or your family's social security numbers in your list of vital information or in online files or folders, no matter how secure they are.

If you have to have those numbers with you (and haven't memorized them), copy or scan the originals and place them in a secure safe deposit box instead.

Print Photos

I don't know about you, but the worst part about watching coverage of tornadoes and earthquakes is the look on victim's faces as they pick through the rubble of their homes, trying to find a keepsake. Even a photo of their wedding or of their children, can mean the difference between being with or without their cherished memories. What a horrible thing it would be, to be left without the pictures you treasure the most, especially when keeping them safe and sound is so easy.

One thing that makes printed photos so much harder to back up is that they need to be scanned before they can be archived. Another is the fact that we get so used to seeing our favorite photos hanging around the house, that we don't always think to take them off the wall while we're scanning the rest for safekeeping.

The third problem is that relatives are notorious for safeguarding family photos, to the point where they won't even let you take the family albums home with you to scan. The good news is, with the advent of portable wand scanners, you can take your scanner with you. The bad news is, you might have to use it under the watchful eye of Aunt Sadie!

Portable wand scanners, like the VuPoint Magic Wand or Pandigital Personal Scanner, have come a long way. They run on batteries or are rechargeable and save anything you scan onto an SD card. The best part about it is that you can scan photos, documents, even things like marriage certificates or historical documents by swiping the scanner over it, instead of having to take all of those documents home and putting them, one at a time, through your scanner. It's especially good, like we said, for scanning photos at relative's homes. If they don't want the photo leaving the house, just take the scanner over and scan the photos you want, even in they're still in the frame or album. It's especially good for fragile photos that are stuck to the album. And if there's more than one on a page, scan the whole page then crop the photos apart later. Photos archived, originals safeguarded!

One other method of scanning that we wanted to mention is the Kodak Personal Scanner. It's a bit different than the others, because you can feed photos into it and it scans them as they pass through an inch thick scanning bed. The interesting part is that it comes with an attachment that feeds negatives and slides into the scanner and – are you ready for this – actually makes a digital copy of the photo, just as if you had taken it to the photo processor.

We actually had some slides that someone had given us, and since we never used slides, we didn't have the equipment to look at them. With the Kodak Scanner, all we did was feed the slide into the scanner and suddenly we had full color, beautiful photos from the sixties, that looked like they were processed yesterday. Absolutely amazing!

So are you ready to preserve your print photos? Great! Let's get to it!

Organized

How To Archive Your Print Photos

Your Mission, Should You Choose To Accept It...

...is to find and archive all of your printed photos, whether they're in albums, picture frames or sitting at the bottom of your kitchen drawer! Any photos that you want to keep safe for yourself and future generations. So let's get started!

Where Are Your Pictures? — 1

First, locate and gather all of your physical photos.

Don't forget to look for all your albums, photos in drawers or files and those hanging in frames on the walls or sitting on your bookshelf. Then you'll decide which of those photos you want to archive for safekeeping.

Which Ones Do I Scan? — 2

Although all of your photos are important, some mean more to you than others.

Separate your photos into two different piles.

In Pile 1, place photos that you want to copy and save in a digital format, for safekeeping.

In Pile 2, place photos that you:
- Already have in digital format and could easily recopy if the one you're holding was harmed or destroyed.
- Have numerous copies of in other locations. Check to make sure that this is actually true, before you decide not to scan them.
- Simply don't care enough about to keep it disaster safe.

You can go ahead and put the photos in the second pile back where you found them.

Here's one of our favorite scanners, the Epson Perfection. It's the only scanner we've ever found that actually restores photos from the 70s and 80s that have turned brown and orange, back to normal with just one button. Amazing!

Scan Away! 3

Scan all of the photos in Pile 1, saving them to your computer. If you have a lot of photos, get the kids involved or throw a scanning party for your relatives, and let them help you scan, then give them a copy of the photos they want to take home with them.

Once you have all of your saved photos in the folder on your computer, copy that folder and save it with a different name, like Photo Archive Backup, with today's date. Place a copy of your backup folder in at least three different locations. For specific instructions on archiving digital photos, see the chapter on Digital Photos.

Safely Storing Print Photos 4

Once you've scanned your photos, **you can place the originals that aren't on display:**
- In a safe deposit box or water/fireproof safe in your own city or with relatives in the city where you'll be evacuating.
- In your watertight Plastic Evacuation Bin. Only place the photos that you actually need to have with you, in this bin. If you'll also have access to copies of photos in your safe deposit box, then don't take any copies with you that you would worry about, if lost.

Digital Photos

With digital photography as inexpensive and easy as it is today, chances are you have more photos of your family and friends than ever before. If you're like most people, all of those photos are sitting on your computer, in a bunch of different folders. Or worse, they're sitting in your camera, just waiting to be accidently erased. And what about your regular print photos – the kind you have in photo albums or frames? At least the digital photos have a chance of being copied and backed up in a few different locations. But if those one-of-a-kind family photos are destroyed, they're gone forever.

Digital or print, all it takes is one fire, flood, fried hard drive or hacked Facebook account and all of those memories are gone, along with a huge piece of your family's history.

In the shortcut sheets that follow, you'll learn some quick and easy tips for downloading and archiving all of your photos – even the ones from your smartphone. First, here are two ways to share photos with your family that you may not know about.

The first is something new from Hewlett Packard called ePrint. You can either use it with an app on your smartphone or tablet, or with most of their wireless enabled all-in-one printers. All you do is email your photo from your camera or smartphone to a special email address, and your photo will be sent directly to your printer. Your picture will be printed and waiting for you when you get home. So, what's the big deal, you say? First so many people leave their photos in their camera or phone so long that they've forgotten that they even have them! So this is a great way to actually use the photos you take. But the cool factor is, you can also send your photos to other people with ePrint, whether or not they have a computer. Andy Lisoskie at HP told us a great story about his grandmother. She doesn't have a computer and even if she did, wouldn't know how to use it. But when he or his relatives take a picture of the kids or a family vacation, they make sure to send the best ones via ePrint to Grandma's printer. All of a sudden, she looks at the printer and all these wonderful photos are waiting for her to admire and stick on the refrigerator. They appear like magic and put her right in the middle of her grandkids lives, even if she can't be there in person.

The second tip we'd like to pass along that has nothing to do with archiving your photo – only about making them better. Have you ever noticed that there's always one person in the family who volunteers to take all the pictures? They're usually the same people who really hate having their picture taken.

We've had a few people like that in our family and now that they're gone, our family has almost no pictures of them. Memories are so important to the next generation and it's up to you to start preserving them today, even if you don't like seeing yourself on film. Years from now, no one is going to care if your left earlobe is longer than your right or that side of your hair always pops up. What they'll want to see – or wish they could see – is you.

Being the photographer in the family is wonderful, but just make sure you turn the camera around on yourself every once in a while and while you're at it, every member of the family, whether they like it or not. Someday someone is going to thank you for it. We guarantee it!

So here are some tips on backing up the photos you already have and safeguarding the ones you'll take in the future, and no we don't mean by uploading them to Instagram!

Organized

How To Archive Your Digital Photos

Your Mission, Should You Choose To Accept It...

Your mission is to make all of your treasured photos completely accessible during a disaster, emergency evacuation, computer or Internet meltdown. Just follow the steps below to locate all of your important photos, scan or copy them and store them in at least **three** secure, damage-proof locations.

1. Where Are Your Pictures?

If you're like most people, your digital photos are in one of two places – sitting on your computer, in a bunch of different folders – or sitting in your camera or phone, just waiting to be accidently erased.

So if you have any photos on your cameras or phones, go get them now and download them to your computer, saving them to the folder where you normally store them.

2. Ready For Backup

Since you're already on your computer, let's back up all of your digital photos.
- First, create a new folder on your computer desktop and name it Backup Photos (dd/mm/yy) using today as the date.
- Then locate the folders that contain all of the digital photos that you want to keep safe. Copy the folders and paste them into the new backup folder, leaving the original files where they are on your computer.
- If you need more detailed instructions on copying and pasting files and folders on your computer, go to the Data section of the book.
- When you're through copying and pasting your folders into the Backup Folder, double check to make sure that there is a copy of your folders in the original location as well as the new location.

3. Photos That Download Themselves? Cool!

By the way, if you regularly have trouble remembering to download your pictures from your phone and camera here are two things that can really help.

For your phone, consider downloading the Dropbox App at www.dropbox.com. It's a free app that will send every photo you take with your phone directly to your computer. For your camera, consider getting a Wi-Fi enabled camera like the Samsung Smart Wi-Fi Camera. Snap a photo and it arrives on your computer. No muss, no fuss.

Safely Storing Digital Photos 4

Where and how you decide to secure and store your photos is up to you. But here are a few ideas. If your photos are digital, **you can place them:**

- On a flash drive or portable hard drive, and take them with you during evacuation on a key ring or in your plastic evacuation bin.
- Place the flash drive or portable hard drive, in a safe deposit box or water/fireproof safe in your own city.
- Place the flash drive or portable hard drive, in a safe deposit box, water/fireproof safe, or with relatives in the city where you'll be evacuating.
- Place the photos on a password-protected online file repository or on the file directory of your family's personal web site. This way, you can retrieve them from any Internet-enabled computer.
- You can also save an extra copy of your photos on Flickr or another internet photo service. But this really shouldn't be your long-term solution, or only solution.

Safely Storing Print Photos 5

If the photos you want to safeguard are prints, or cherished originals, **you can place them:**
In a safe deposit box or water/fireproof safe in your own city.

- In a safe deposit box, water/fireproof safe, or with relatives in the city where you'll be evacuating.
- In your watertight Plastic Evacuation Bin. Only place the photos that you actually need to have with you, in this bin. If you'll also have access to copies of photos in your safe deposit box, then don't take any copies with you that you would worry about, if lost.

For more instructions on storing or safeguarding your print photos, see the Print Photos section of this book.

Home Videos and Home Movies

Videos just aren't like any other keepsakes.

Photos, MP3s and important documents, can be tossed onto a computer or a portable hard drive and taken with us in an emergency. Yes digital videos are just as easy to archive, but if you're like us, the videos that we treasure most are on videocassettes or 8mm film. Try taking those with you in an evacuation!

And that's not the only problem. With video cameras and smartphones as inexpensive and easy to use as they are today, chances are that you have more videos of you, your family and friends than ever before. And they're probably sitting on your camera, your phone or on Facebook, just waiting to be accidently deleted.

Your goal for this section is to make all of your treasured home movies, films and videos safe, sound and completely accessible to you during a disaster, computer or Internet meltdown.

Organized

How To Archive Your Home Movies & Videos

Your Mission, Should You Choose To Accept It...

...is to find and archive all of your home movies, be they videos, DVDs, Super 8s or any other kind of format. Anything that you want to keep safe for yourself and future generations. So let's get started!

1. You Can't Archive Them If You Can't Find Them

Grab a pencil and paper and jot down the types of videos you want to **secure**, what format they're in (digital, standard video cassette, DVD or special format video cassette) and their current location.

Using the list you just compiled, **locate** and **gather** all of those videos set them aside for a moment.

2. Any Videos Lurking On Your Hard Drive?

Do you have any home videos on your computer?

Yes? Then let's start with them. And while you're at it, grab your video camera and cell phone so you can download any videos that are still there.

- Create one new folder on your computer desktop and name it Backup Videos (dd/mm/yy) with today's date.
- Locate all of the digital home videos on your computer. Leaving all the original files where they are, copy each one into the new Backup folder.
- Instead of taking the time to choose which videos you want to keep safe and which you don't really care about, it's much easier just to copy and back them all up right now. Then some time when you have nothing better to do, you can sort through them.
- If you need more detailed instructions on copying and pasting files and folders on your computer, see the section on How To Use This Book.

3. Now For The Super 8s & Videocassettes

Now it's time to deal with your 8mm or Super 8 films and video cassettes. Take a few moments to gather them and separate them into two different piles.

In Pile 1, place any videos that you want to copy and save in a digital format.

In Pile 2, place videos that you:
- Already have in digital format and could easily recopy if the one you're holding were harmed or destroyed.
- Have numerous other copies of the video in other locations. (Check to make sure that this is actually so before you decide not to copy them)
- Simply don't care enough about to keep it disaster safe.
- Go ahead and put the videos in the second pile back where you found them.

The Best Way To Copy Videos — 4

The only way to archive your films and videos is to copy or transfer them into a digital format and save them to your computer or onto a DVD. There are a few great ways to do this yourself or you can have a professional do it. If your movies are on videocassette, ION makes a great little device called a Video 2 PC Analog To Digital USB Video Converter for your PC or Mac. It's a small device -- you plug one end into your computer and the other end into your VCR and it saves your videos in digital format on your computer.

What About My Super 8 Movies? — 5

If you have reels of 8mm &Super 8 films lying around, you'll need to have them transferred to digital format professionally.

There's a wonderful company called iMemories (www.imemories.com) that helped us digitize our movies. They'll even send you a safe ship kit equipped with a GPS locator to pinpoint your movies' exact location, every step of the way. And they do an incredible job of transferring film, videotapes, audio files and photos. The best part is that once they're completed, you can share them with your friends and relatives in your own private online theater.

Finding Buried Treasure — 6

You know when you're watching a video and you see that perfect moment? Your kid finally hangs ten perfectly on her skateboard or you nail that dive with a 10.0 rip right into the water. What if you could capture that moment in an extraordinary still photo, right from the video?

Better still, what if you could turn a moment that you only had on video or in a home movie, into a photograph? Now you can. With an amazing app called Perfect Pic, you can turn any frame of any video into a crystal clear photo.

We used it to create still photos out of moments that had been long buried on 8mm film. For more information and a quick tutorial on how to get great results using it, check out our blog post.
http://rnn10.wordpress.com/2013/09/02/capturingperfectmoment/

Music

So how much is your music collection worth?

And more importantly, how much is it worth to you?

The other day I walked into a store and wasn't thinking about anything but finding what I needed. All of a sudden "Hooked On A Feeling," which will be forever known as the Dancing Baby song from "Ally McBeal," began to play on the store radio. Not only did the song have my immediate attention, but now I had a huge smile on my face just picturing that ridiculous dancing baby. So did half of the people in the store!

What is it about music that gives us such immediate, overwhelming emotions? It just transports us back in time to a moment or a memory. I think that's why people never want to part with their music, no matter how old it is. It's not just music. It's the soundtrack of our lives.

So let's make sure that your soundtrack is there for you to listen to and enjoy for years to come.

And when you're done, not only will you be able to find your songs when you want them, but you'll finally be able to listen to that amazing vinyl jazz solo on your iPod!

Organized

How To Archive Your Favorite Albums & Cassettes

Your Mission, Should You Choose To Accept It...

...is to take all of your favorite music – CDs, cassettes or vinyl albums and turn them into MP3s, then back them up to your computer and other safe locations. That way, not only will you be able listen to all your favorite old music on your smartphone or MP3 player, but you'll be able to keep all those songs you love safe for years to come.

1. Where Is All Your Music Hiding?

Grab a pencil and paper and jot down the types of music you have that you want to **secure** and their current location.

Using the list you just compiled, **locate** and **gather** all of the CDs, cassettes and vinyl albums that you want to secure and set them aside for a moment.

2. What About My Digital Music?

Do you have MP3 or other digital music files? First grab your MP3 player, your cell phone, your iPad or tablets and make sure all of those music files are downloaded to your computer desktop now.
- Create one new folder on your computer desktop and name it "Backup Music (dd/mm/yy)" with today's date.
- Locate all of the digital music on your hard drive that you want to keep safe. Leave the original files where they are on your computer, but copy each one and place the copies in that new Backup folder.

3. Time To Deal With The Albums & CDs

Although all of your music is important, some means more to you than others. Take a few moments to look at your CDs, cassettes and vinyl albums, and separate them into two different piles.
- In the first pile, place music that you'll need to copy and save in a digital format, to keep them safe.
- In the second pile, place music that you:
    - Already have in digital format.
    - Have numerous other copies of the music in other locations. (be sure that this is actually so before you decide not to copy them)
    - Simply don't care enough about to keep it disaster safe.
- You can go ahead and put the music in the second pile away.

Convert Your CDs to MP3s — 4

You can convert CDs right on your computer, using your computer's music software. For a PC, that would be Windows Media Player.

Just put the CD into your computer and the software will automatically pop up. Follow the instructions to "rip" your CD.

When your songs are ripped, take your CD out and save the new MP3 files to the music folder on your computer. We'll back those up to keep them safe in a few minutes. And don't forget to add those new songs to your iPod or MP3 player!

Convert Cassettes & Albums To MP3s — 5

Here are a few easy ways we've found to convert your cassettes or albums to MP3s.

There are several vinyl album to MP3 recorders available including the Crosley Memory Master II 3-Speed Turntable with CD Player/Recorder. The nice thing about that one is that it converts cassettes and vinyl to CD or to MP3s.

And if you only have cassettes to convert, there is the ION Tape Express.

Save Them To Your Computer — 6

Download the new MP3 files to your computer desktop, placing them in a brand new folder. When you're finished, make one copy of that complete folder. Place the original folder in with the other digital music files on your computer. Then place the copy of the folder into the backup folder you created earlier.

If you don't have access to a converter or don't own a computer, then have a relative or friend convert them and store them for you. And don't forget to talk to your older relatives about archiving their music. They might really appreciate having you put the music from their old vinyl, cassettes or CDs on an MP3 player that they can listen to.

And Archive The Back Up Copies — 7

Where and how you decide to secure and store your own digital music files is up to you. But here are a few ideas:
- On a password-protected flash drive or portable hard drive, and take them with you during evacuation on a key ring or in your plastic evacuation bin.
- On a password-protected flash drive or portable hard drive, in a safe deposit box or water/fireproof safe in your own city.
- On a password-protected flash drive or portable hard drive, in a safe deposit box, water/fireproof safe, or with relatives in the city where you'll be evacuating.
- In a password-protected online file repository or on the file directory of your family's personal web site. This way you can retrieve them from any Internet-enabled computer.

Family Recipes

How many recipes do you have sitting around your house? Hundreds? Thousands?

And let me guess. Some are in a recipe box, some stuck in the back of a drawer, a few are on your computer and the rest are boxed up in an attic or a musty basement.

What is it about recipes that makes them so hard to manage?

We think it's probably the fact that they come in so many different shapes and sizes. It makes them so hard to organize, let alone archive them for safekeeping.

The other problem – how in the world do you classify them?

There are the recipes that you tear out of a magazine because they sound good, but have never tried. The recipes that you love but never make, because they're mixed in the drawer with the ones you've never tried. The ones that you really treasure, written in your grandmother or great grandmother's handwriting. And finally, there are your family favorites, that may not be on a recipe card at all because you just prepare them from memory.

You see where we're going with this. It's time to cut right through that organized chaos of yours and get your most important recipes backed up for posterity. That's why we're only going to deal with two types of recipes for this exercise -- the ones that you cherish or the family favorites that you use all the time.

The rest? Well, they can wait to be sorted until the next rainy day.

Here are the steps to archive your recipes, along with some wonderful ways to share them with your family, your children and your grandchildren.

Organized

How To Archive Your Family's Favorite Or Treasured Recipes

Your Mission, Should You Choose To Accept It...

...is to make all of your treasured recipes completely safe and secure during a disaster, emergency evacuation, computer or Internet meltdown.

1. Where Are Those Recipes Of Yours?

Grab a pencil and paper and jot down the types of recipes you want to **secure** and their current location.

Remember, we're only going to be dealing with two types of recipes for this exercise -- the ones that you cherish or the family favorites that you use all the time. The rest can wait for a rainy day, when you have the time to sort them all out.

2. We Gather Together...

Using the list you just compiled, **locate** and **gather** all of the printed recipes that you want to secure and set them aside for a moment.

3. Recipes Already On Your Computer

Are any of your recipes already on the computer? If they are, let's start with them. Otherwise, just go to the next step.
- Create one new folder on your computer desktop and name it "Backup Recipes (dd/mm/yy)" with today's date.
- Locate all of the digital recipe files that you want to keep safe. Leave the original files where they are on your computer, but copy each one and place the copies in your new Backup Folder.

4. Scanning The Rest

Scan each handwritten recipe and download it to your computer, placing it in the Backup Recipe Folder you just created. When you're finished, make one copy of that complete folder and place it with your photo or video files – wherever you keep things on your computer that are important to you.

There are several great ways to scan your recipes.
- If you use a regular scanner, being sure to scan both sides of the recipe it in the same file so you don't lose half the recipe.
- If the recipe cards are fragile, try a scanner like the Kodak Personal Scanner. It comes with a special plastic housing for fragile prints or documents, that protect the documents as it guides them safely through the rollers.
- If the recipe cards you want to scan are being held captive by a relative, just get a portable wand scanner, take it over to their house and scan them right there. That way the originals will never even leave their possession!

Keeping Them Safe — 5

After you've scanned or printed your recipes, store them in at least **three** secure, damage-proof locations. That way if one or two of the locations are inaccessible, you'll still be able to have all your recipes at your fingertips.

Recipes With Memories Attached — 6

While you're going through your special recipes, jot down all the details you can remember about them -- memories, anecdotes, family stories -- then save them along with the recipe.

Now you're not just sharing a great recipe, you're passing down a memory.

With A Side Of Video — 7

Grab a video camera and have someone tape you making your family's favorite dishes, then go over to your mom's, grandma's or aunt's house and capture them making that special cake or world-class spaghetti.

Maybe she'll even throw in some juicy family stories!

Family Favorites Packaged To Go — 8

Want a cool way to share your favorite recipes with your whole family? Why not make a recipe book?

Drug stores, copy shops or publishing websites like Lulu.com have incredibly easy-to-use services you can use to turn your favorite recipes into your very own book.

It can be inexpensive or pricey depending on the length and binding, but it's a great way to share your family's favorite recipes and memories.

Family History

Every family has a history keeper.

Sometimes it's the eldest daughter or the most responsible aunt and sometimes it's simply the person with the biggest house. But in every family throughout the centuries, the task of keeping the family history alive, usually falls to one person. It doesn't even matter if that person is particularly good at it. Whether they use a basement or an attic, there's always one person whose home is piled with photo albums, birth certificates, marriage certificates, newspaper clippings and Civil War muskets.

And for centuries that made sense. Families didn't move a lot, and photos and keepsakes – well it was so difficult to make copies of them or move them without them falling to pieces – that it was smart to leave them be.

Which was fine until something happened to the history keeper's house. I can't tell you how many times we've heard the same story. "Aunt Sadie had a huge house so she kept all the family albums. We never thought about whether they were safe or not, until the night her house burned down or her basement flooded. And then suddenly, two hundred years of history was a soggy, unsalvageable mass of lumpy paper."

And we're not just talking about historical documents. History is also passed down to the next generation through storytelling by people who had heard them told so many times, they could simply sit down by the fire and regale everyone with tales of Uncle Frank's escapades during the war.

That's why doing an oral history of your family is such a great idea. Years ago, families didn't have sound on their 8 mm or Super8 movies, and never had the chance to hear what their great or great-great grandparents sounded like. It's such an honor and such an opportunity to be able to capture all of the people we love on video now so that we can share them with generations to come. Not only does it bring history to life for everyone, but it shows the entire journey of who we are as a family and how that has made us the individuals we are today.

When Spike Lee was on NBC's "Who Do You Think You Are," he told a touching story about his grandmother. Evidently she was a wonderful storyteller and lived way into her nineties. Even though he's a filmmaker and had all of the equipment right there at his fingertips, he just never got around to getting her or her stories on film. And then she passed away, and he lost that opportunity. He had tears in his eyes when he told the story on the show, and today, not getting her on film is one of his biggest regrets. Maybe he just didn't want to think that some time she might no longer be with them. So take Spike Lee's advice.

Grab a video camera and get those relatives and their stories on video for posterity. Then anytime you or your children want to hear Grandma or Great-Grandpa and visit with them for a bit, all you have to do is pop in the video and they and their stories will spring to life.

So going back to the question we posed earlier, who is the best person to be the keeper of the history in your family? There's only one good answer to that question.

Everyone!

Every person in every family should share the load by sharing the pieces of its history.

And here's how to do it.

Organized

How To Archive Your Family History

Your Mission, Should You Choose To Accept It...

...is to back up and then archive all of your family history, documentation, family trees and historical keepsakes, not only to keep it safe, but to be able to share it with all the other members of your family.

Speaking Of Family History — 1

Grab a pencil and paper and jot down the types of family history documentation you currently have in your home.

Here are a few ideas to get you started:
- Family Photos
- Family Tree
- Relatives' Birth/Marriage/Death Certificates
- Land Titles/Deeds
- Family History Documents
- Census Records
- Relatives' Videos/Interviews/Oral Histories on tape
- Anything else related to the history of your family except for photos, which we'll handle in the section on Print Photos.

A Little Detective Work — 2

Using the list you just compiled, **locate** and **gather** all of those documents. If there are many documents, divide them into separate piles, one for each family surname.

The best way to safeguard these important documents and artifacts is to scan them and save them to your computer. Open the Backup Folder you already have on your hard drive from previous sections and save them in a new folder called "Family History".

Documents That Are Already Digitized — 3

Are any of the family history documents or photos you located already on computer?

Yes? Copy the documents (leaving the originals where they are on your computer) and place them in your new "Family History" backup folder

No? Continue with the next section.

Keeping Your Documents Safe — 4

Print, scan or make three copies of the documents or other materials you located, and store them in at least **three** secure, damage-proof locations on your computer, your portable hard drive and safe deposit boxes. That way if one or two of the locations are inaccessible, you'll still be able to grab the information you need.

For suggestions on the best locations for your archived files and documents see "Before You Begin," at the beginning of the book.

Finding Branches Of The Family Tree — 5

If you want to take your family history up a notch – or if you're the historian in your family, start a family tree or get a membership at Ancestry.com. In fact, just choose the family member who is the best researchers and put them hot on the trail of your forefathers and mothers.

And if you want to take it one step further, try Family Tree Maker software to create your own piece of living history that you can share with other family members.

Scoping Out Aunt Sophie's House — 6

Once you begin preserving your family history, don't forget to look for the missing pieces of it at your relative's homes. There must be someone in your family who has boxes of it in their attic or basement.

And Putting It All On DVD — 7

Gather all of the family history and photos from all your family member's homes and have a scanning party. You can share memories while you scan and then when you're done, copy all of the documents and photos onto a nicely labeled DVD for each person to take home. You can do the same thing with the family videos or Super8 movies. One group can be scanning photographs and documents , while another group transfers the videos and films onto DVDs.

Don't Forget The Sound — 8

Years ago, families didn't have sound on their 8 mm or Super8 movies, which means many people never had the chance to hear what their great or great-great grandparents sounded like.

So next time you have a family gathering, grab a video camera and get those wonderful faces and voices on video for posterity. And if they're willing, don't be shy about asking them to share their favorite stories or memories. Then years from now, all you'll have to do is pop in a video and visit with them any time you and your children want.

Voice Mails or Special Recordings That You Want to Keep

You've got to love voicemail.

It's fast, it's convenient and it's everywhere from your cell phone to your landline. Gone are the days when you would walk in the door, play the messages on the answering machine, reset it and replace the tape when it inevitably breaks. Yes voicemail is great. That is, until your phone company decides that saved message of yours has been sitting on their server long enough and deletes it.

Not a big deal for people who don't mind a little electronic housekeeping. But it's a huge deal for people who want, or need to keep a treasured message!

For thousands of people, that saved recording is the last greeting, message or voice of a person that they love.

A friend of ours kept her husband's cell phone account active after he unexpectedly passed away, so her grown children could hear his voice on the greeting anytime they wanted. Not really the best way to preserve it.

In fact, we heard a story about a Chicago woman who lost her son in an accident and decided to keep his final message to her, saved on her phone so she could play it to make herself feel better when she was having a bad day. Even though she carefully re-saved that message on her voicemail every two weeks, one day her carrier changed software and inadvertently erased it. She was heartbroken. Weeks later, after scouring their system, the cell phone carrier finally found the message and sent it to her as an MP3 file.

Do you have treasured messages lurking on your answering machine or voicemail? Here are the best ways to preserve them.

Organized

How To Save Your Treasured Voice Mail Messages

What Do You Mean By Treasured Voice Mail Messages?

For thousands of people, a saved voicemail isn't just taking up space on their cell phone or answering machine. It's a message with the voice of the person that they love, speaking to them for what might have been the last time.

If you have a recording that is THAT important, you can't just leave it up to chance, hoping that it never gets erased. And backing it up is so easy to do, you'll wonder why you didn't do it months ago!

If The Message Is On An Answering Machine — 1

If the message is on an **answering machine that uses a cassette tape**, the easiest way to archive it is to simply save the tape.

But when a message is THIS important, you should also back up the cassette tape by recording the message as an MP3 and saving it to a few different locations on your computer as well. Our favorite tool to use to back up cassettes is the ION Tape Express. You can find it on Amazon at this link: http://amzn.to/1U8OMmT.

Or A Machine With A Digital Chip... — 2

If the message is on an **answering machine with a digital chip**, play the message and record it onto a digital recorder, cassette or directly to your computer, using Sound Recorder (Windows/PC) or QuickTime (Mac), to make it into an MP3 that you can keep for posterity.

If The Message Is On Voicemail — 4

If the message is on **voicemail,** you can use any type of digital recorder to back it up and turn it into an MP3. Follow the directions on your specific recorder, but generally all you'll have to do is connect the recorder to your cell phone to the recorder.

You'll place one end in the earphone jack of your phone to the microphone (in) jack of your recorder, play the message and record it to your digital recorder. Then save it to your PC as an MP3 for safekeeping.

Leaving It To The Professionals 5

If you'd rather leave the archiving to the professionals, go to www.cbwproductions.com. They'll make a copy of any message that's on your cell phone voice mail and email you the MP3 copy or if you would rather, send it to you on a CD.

The next time someone leaves you a message that you never want to lose, do yourself a favor. Take five minutes to back it up.

How to Make Your Breakable Keepsakes More Disaster Resistant

There once was a man who was so afraid of earthquakes that he did everything he possibly could to prepare for one. He had water, food and first aid kits lining the walls of his ocean-front home. Even his bookcases and cabinets were carefully bolted to the wall and he made sure that everyone in his home knew where to go when "the big one" hit.

Then one morning the big one came. He and his family ran into the spots they had practiced, into doorways, under the heavy tables. It seemed like an eternity before the rumbling stopped. When it did, they looked at each other, scared but smiling. They'd done it! They were okay. They had food, they had shelter – this wasn't so bad.

The man rushed to the door followed by his family. The sun was shining, and they were thrilled to be alive. Until they heard a deafening roar. And then they spotted it. A ten-foot wave headed right at them. They ran up the street, up the hill as fast as they could. They made it to the top just in time to watch the water swallow up their neighborhood, their home and along with it, all their supplies. The man looked at his wife and said, "That was strange. I never saw that coming."

Just because you're ready for what you <u>think</u> might happen, doesn't mean you're ready for something you would never expect in a million years.

Here are some tips to keep the breakable or non-water resistant keepsakes that you love, safe and secure during earthquakes, hurricanes and other destructive disasters.

- Prepare your collectibles and keepsakes ahead of time by creating an inventory of items that are emotionally, financially or historically valuable to you and your family, so that you know which items need to be secured. If you have any documentation on the items, such as ownership papers, authentication or appraisals, copy them and place them with your home inventory. And don't forget to keep copies of the photos and documentation in another city as well as your own, for safekeeping in case of a regional emergency.
- Remember that anchoring breakable items down so they don't break during an earthquake, not only protects your collectibles from breakage, but it also protects you and your family AFTER the earthquake. Broken items like crystal, glassware, collectibles, and ceramics can make it hazardous for you to get out of your home or to move around safely to get things back in order.

- Strap down tall furniture so it can't topple over. Carol Burnett once told a story about the Northridge Earthquake. She always slept on the same side of the bed – in fact she didn't even bother turning down the other side. The night of the quake, for some reason, she couldn't sleep and tossed and turned so much that she ended up on the other side of the bed. As the quake started to shake her home, an unanchored television set from the bookcase beside her flew out of the bookcase and landed right on the side of the bed where she normally would been lying. Talk about a close call! And it could have been prevented by simply strapping her TV to the bookcase and anchoring the bookcase to the wall.
- Small fragile collectibles and keepsakes can not only break in an earthquake or storm, but they can easily become sharp flying projectiles that can seriously harm family members and pets. Place them in a cabinet with doors that close. Then make sure that they are secured to the shelf and back of the cabinet with QuakeHold Museum Wax, an inexpensive putty-like substance museums use to secure objects to shelves without harming the object. And while you're at it, make sure that the cabinet itself is secured to the wall so that it will be more resistant to shaking.
- Put keepsakes where you can get to them easily. You don't want to be running around during a tornado warning or wildfire trying to find Great-Grandma's crystal vase!
- Do you have a great deal of vital personal or business documents that must be kept safe? SentrySafe makes file cabinets that are fireproof, waterproof, and crushproof – basically capable of withstanding a 30-foot drop. The cabinets come with high-security locks designed to withstand picking and drilling. The only downside is that they're very expensive, but for a business, or for people who must keep critical documents safe, it could be well worth the investment.
- If you live in an area with a regular disaster season – like hurricane or wildfire season, consider placing your breakable keepsakes in a safe deposit box or in your evacuation location during disaster season. In an area prone to flooding, place valuables on a high shelf above any previous water marks.
- And if you have a wine collection – whether it is just a few bottles or a room full – check out QuakeGuardian wine bottle fasteners. Created to safely secure wine bottles in their wine racks for earthquakes up to 8.0, QuakeGuardian is quickly becoming the fastener of choice for wine connoisseurs worldwide.

How to Keep From Losing or Destroying Your Cell Phone

Whether your cell phone is just a phone to you or a little mobile assistant that holds all of your most critical information, you'll probably agree that losing your phone would be a major pain.

Cell phones and smartphones are basically our links to the outside world. It wasn't as much of a problem a few years ago to lose one, because we all had landlines, or office phones, or jobs that actually didn't depend on constant access to email, voicemail and the internet. But now, losing, dropping or otherwise destroying your phone is tantamount to putting yourself temporarily out of order!

Here are a few ways to keep from losing or destroying your cell phone.

Zomm, The Digital Leash For Your Cell Phone

The two things we love most about cell phones are the two things that make them most vulnerable. They're small and mobile. How many times a day do you see someone walking around holding their phone in their hand? They're not talking or texting, they're just holding it. Until they go to pick up something else. Then they put it down. And walk away… Without it. Not that _you_ would ever do something like that, right?

Fortunately, now there is a way for your phone to tell _you_ where _it_ is! It's called Zomm. Zomm is a poker chip-sized device that's a virtual leash for your cell phone. All you do is put your Zomm on your keychain and if you go more than ten feet away from your phone – or if it "goes" ten feet away from you – it lets out a loud alert to remind you to go back and grab it ASAP. It's also great if someone helps themselves to your phone! Kind of like giving your phone a way to call for help.

And that's not all Zomm can do. With the Zomm car kit, it also becomes a hands-free speakerphone and an emergency panic button. Just a push of the button summons 911 or a pre-programmed emergency number like your spouse or your friend.

Find My iPhone or iPad App From Apple

With Find My iPhone, one of Apple's most popular apps, if you misplace your iPhone or iPad, you can send a signal to your misplaced device, to have it send out a signal so you can locate it, the moment you realize it's missing. With the GPS locator built into the app, you can also find the phone via your Mac or iPad. And if the phone has been stolen, the app also includes a way to immediately wipe it of all information and disable it. Crisis averted, thanks to Find My iPhone!

Dry-All Wet Cellular Phone Emergency Kits

Have you ever dropped your phone in water? We haven't, thank goodness, but we sure have a lot of friends who have, and it can be a nightmare! People have as many tricks to dry out a waterlogged phone as there are types of cell phones. But no matter how sure your best friend is that her method works best, there is one tried and true way to bring a drowned phone back to life.

It's called Dry-All and it's a special drying kit for cell phones, smartphones and even tablets. There are different kits for different types of phones so if you or your spouse has a tendency to drop phones into water, you should probably keep one or two kits for your particular brand and size of phone on hand. All you do is drop the phone or device into the bag and the Dry-All material, dries it out bringing nearly every wet phone back to life.

Lookout Phone Backup

The Lookout Mobile Security App, which works with Android and BlackBerry smartphones, can help you locate a missing phone via an onscreen map or lock your phone if it's lost or stolen. You can also use it to back up the contacts on your phone and if you lose your phone or if it crashes, you can simply transfer all of your contacts to your new phone.

Yourself & Your Family

Vital Documents

Why do people make such a big deal of having copies of their vital documents at their fingertips? After all, they can easily be replaced by whatever company or government office gave them to you in the first place. Right?

Don't count on it.

Just look at the last few years. After countless tornadoes and hurricanes like Superstorm Sandy, residents returned to find their homes destroyed. Once they began to piece their lives back together, they realized they needed copies of transcripts, birth certificates and other vital documents, but when they went down to their government offices or schools, many of them were underwater or destroyed, along with all of the paper based records that had not yet been digitized. You can't count on your city to replace your records when they have just as good a chance of having their own copies destroyed in the same disaster.

That's why we always suggest that people scan all of their vital documents and keep them in at least three different locations. The originals and hard copies go into a locked file cabinet at home, at the office or in a safe deposit box, while digital copies go onto a portable hard drive and into a safe deposit box in your own city and one in another city, preferably in the location where you and your family would relocate during an city-wide evacuation.

When a document is important enough to keep, make sure you have paper copies and electronic copies in multiple locations. That way no matter what happens, you've done everything that you can to ensure its safety and longevity.

Here's how to do it.

Organized

How To Archive Your Vital Documents

Your Mission, Should You Choose To Accept It...

...is to locate, scan and archive all of your and your family's vital documents, not only to keep them safe, but to have them at your fingertips whenever and wherever you need them, even if you're away from home.

1. Your Vital Documents

Grab a pencil and paper and jot down all of the vital documents you have in your home for each member of your family. Here are a few ideas to get you started.

- ID: Driver's license/State ID, company or school ID, Medicare/Medicaid and other insurance cards.
- Social security cards, social security/retirement or other benefit documents.
- Birth, marriage or divorce certificates.
- School enrollment records, immunization, transcripts and contact information for schools.
- Keys and information for safe deposit boxes.
- Proof of insurance and ownership for your vehicles and other property.
- Deeds, mortgage and contact information for your mortgage company and payment information.
- If you are a landlord, contact information for your tenants, copies of leases, applications and payment information.

2. Gathering All Of Your Documents

Using the list you just compiled, **locate** and **gather** all of those documents.

3. Documenting Your Information

Grab your Financial & Insurance Form (it's in the forms you downloaded earlier in this book) and fill in information on any of the documents you've found that are detailed on the form. You'll complete the rest of the form in the Financial and Insurance sections of this book.

Be sure to include the information that goes along with the documents, like passwords or contact information. For example, your passport number, the contact information for your landlord, the key location or password for your safe deposit box. If necessary, add additional lines to the form to fit it in.

When you're finished, save the form to your computer.

4. Making Your Vital Docs Accessible

Create a new folder on your computer desktop and name it "Backup Vital Documents (dd/mm/yy)," with today's date.

Scan all of the vital documents and save them to the new folder along with your Vital Documents form.

Keeping Your Information Safe

5

Copy and store that folder in at least **three** secure, damage-proof locations on your computer, your portable hard drive and safe deposit boxes. That way if one or two of the locations are inaccessible, you'll still be able to grab the information you need.

DO NOT put your or your family's social security numbers in your list of vital information, or in online files or folders, no matter how secure they are. If you have to have those numbers with you (and haven't memorized them), copy the originals and place the copies in a secure safe deposit box instead. If you need that information during an emergency or evacuation, wait to retrieve it until you can access it on your computer or portable hard drive in your secure location.

For suggestions on the best locations for your archived files and documents see "Before You Begin," at the beginning of the book.

Contacts and Address Books

Tracy and I had been friends since high school. She and her family were so much fun – a husband and two adorable little kids, four-year-old Jennifer and two-year-old Garrett. She prided herself on keeping up with all of her friends and loved having all of us around her. One of her favorite things was her address book, where she kept all of her names and numbers. This was back in the days before everyone had PCs and cell phones at their fingertips. Since all of our friends were in their twenties and thirties, the hardest part was keeping up with everyone's new addresses and phone numbers. One graduates from college, another marries and buys a home. As much as she tried, the book became a maze of different inks and cross outs, but she couldn't bring herself to buy a new one. What was the point when it would just end up in the same shape as the old one a few months later?

One night after spending the day helping a friend, Tracy was driving home alone, when her car was struck by a drunk driver. She was killed instantly.

Her husband was beside himself and when faced with the task of pulling together a funeral, didn't know where to begin. He figured that he would start with Tracy's address book. He'd seen her use it hundreds of times, but now that he desperately needed it, it was nowhere to be found. He and the kids tore the house apart – nothing. The friends and neighbors who lived nearby, couldn't find it either.

At least thirty of us didn't learn that Tracy had passed away until weeks later, when the book finally turned up. We missed her funeral simply because her address book wasn't in a place that her husband could easily find it. And when he did find it, he had trouble figuring out which entries were the most recent, or which of the hundred people, Tracy would have wanted him to notify first.

Here's how to keep that tragedy from happening to your family or friends.

Organized

How To Keep Your Contacts Up To Date

Your Mission, Should You Choose To Accept It...

...is to get your personal contacts organized, accessible and backed up for safe keeping. If you keep your contacts on your computer and have trouble keeping up with them, this how-to sheet is for you!

1. Hunting Down Those Scraps Of Paper

Grab all of those slips of paper, you've been keeping, with your friend's updated phone numbers and emails . And don't forget the addresses you tore off the Christmas card envelopes & the notes at the bottom of your purse.

Now get over to your computer and start updating your contacts.

2. Keeping Your Contacts Up To Date

Outlook or other computer based contacts are the easiest to maintain – but if you maintain them.

Every time you notice that a friend has updated information, take two seconds to update their entry in your contacts.

3. ...Or Once A Month

If you don't have time for two second updates, here's a great way to get them all done.

- Create a new folder on your computer desktop named "Contacts".
- Every time a friend sends you an email with updated contact info, or a new contact, save it and drop it into the folder.
- You can also simply create a Word document and save all those bits of information on that one page.
- Then on the day of your "appointment" make all the changes to your contacts, then delete the info in the folder or the entries on the Word document and start the month fresh.

4. Don't Keep The Location To Yourself

When a friend of ours died suddenly, her husband couldn't find her address book, making him unable to notify a number of people about her death or invite them to her memorial service – us included.

Once your book is updated, tell your spouse, roommate, or if you live alone, your Mom or best friend, where you keep your address book, in case of emergency.

The Conversation 5

Have a quick conversation with your spouse, best friend or parent about which people you would want them to notify if you were seriously injured.

You can also create a "notify" category in your contacts and put each person you'd want to notify of an accident or serious illness, in that category.

That way all your spouse, friend or parent would have to do is sort by the notify category and would instantly have a list of people to notify.

And be sure to have the same conversation with your spouse and parents so that you know who to notify if the situation were reversed.

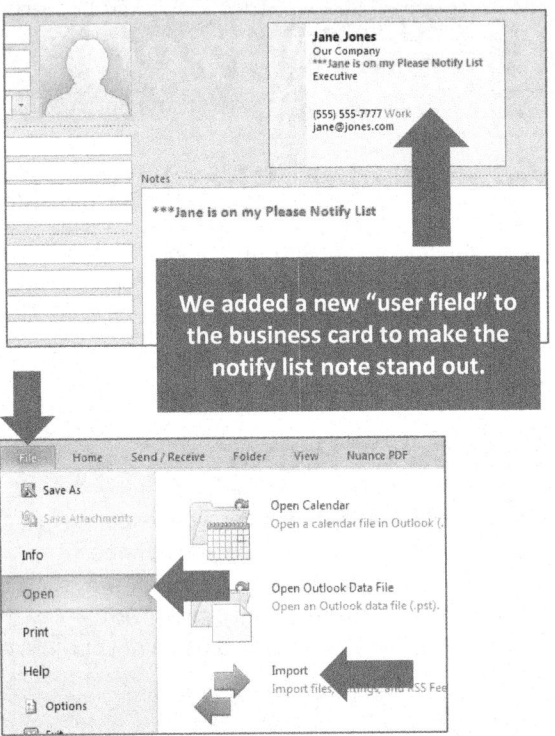

We added a new "user field" to the business card to make the notify list note stand out.

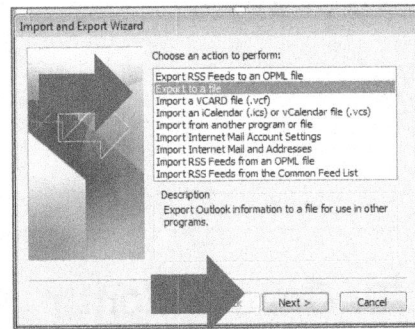

What's Next? 6

- If you haven't already, make sure that your paycheck is direct deposited into your account.
- Find out if your company has any programs or resources for employees who experience disasters/emergencies and how to take advantage of them, if you should ever need to.
- Consider creating a few more streams of income, like starting a small internet business or becoming a paid consultant, to make sure that you have additional income flowing in, in case your current employer is impacted by the same emergency you are.

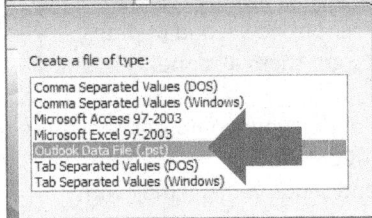

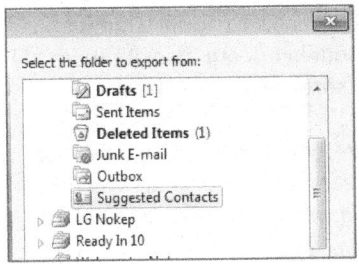

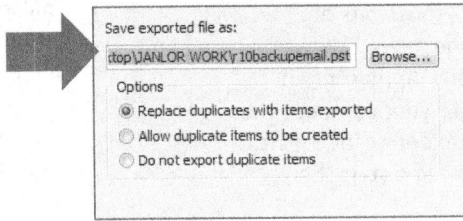

Location, Location, Location 7

While you're at it, save an additional copy onto a portable hard drive or flash drive and put it in a safe deposit box with your other vital documents. That way you'll be able to access your contacts in case your home is inaccessible in an emergency.

Facebook & LinkedIn Contacts

So how many friends do <u>you</u> have on Facebook?

What about connections on LinkedIn or followers on Twitter? A few? Hundreds? Thousands? And how long did it take you to assemble that amazing group of people? A long, long time.

Imagine getting up tomorrow morning, grabbing a cup of coffee and turning on your computer. You double click on the internet icon to sign on to Facebook or LinkedIn and instead of your profile, you get a nice friendly screen inviting you to join. A few minutes of intense panic later, you realize your account has been deleted. Now the stress really kicks in. Not just because it's taken you all that time and effort to cultivate your connections and get your profile just right, but because you just realized something.

You'll never remember the names of all of the people you're no longer linked to!

Just take a deep breath. That nightmare didn't really happen and all of your connections are safe. Even though we can't guarantee you'll never be unceremoniously dumped and forgotten by any of these social sites, at least you'll know who your friends were – uh I mean, are.

Here's how to keep them safe and secure.

Organized

How To Back Up Your Facebook & LinkedIn Account Information

Your Mission, Should You Choose To Accept It...

...is to download and backup your Friends List, photos, videos, posts, messages and other information from Facebook and your contact information from LinkedIn. That way, no matter what happens, even a hiccup in the servers, the contacts you worked so hard to build will be safe and sound on your hard drive.

1. I Can Download My Friends List? Really?

Yes, you really can! Using the instructions below, you can download a lot of the information in your Facebook account, including:
- Your Friends List
- Your Contact Information,
- Interests,
- Groups,
- Photos and Videos that you have uploaded to your account.
- Messages that you have sent and received.

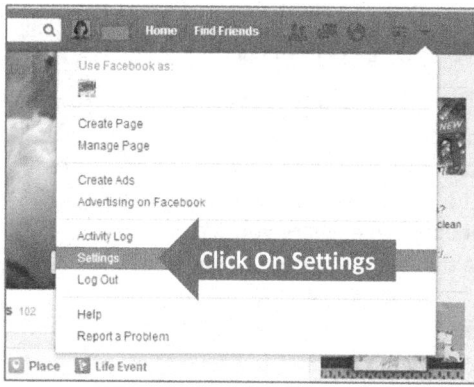

2. First, Go To Account Settings

Just log into your Facebook account, and click on the **Down Arrow** on the right side of your **Account Menu** and choose **Settings**.

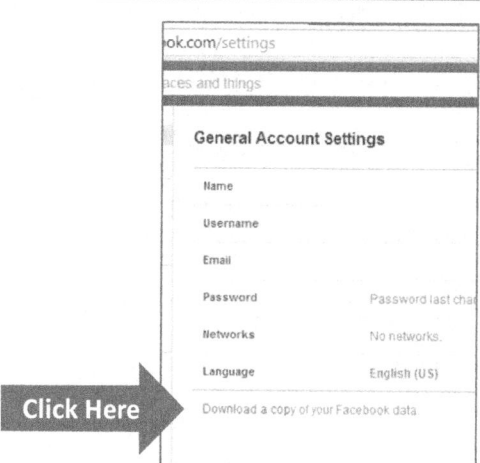

3. Then Download Your Information

1. Click on **Download A Copy** of your Facebook Data
2. Follow the prompts to **enter your password** and then **Download the Archive** of your Facebook Data to your **computer**.

Now That You Have The Information... 4

As Facebook suggests, since this download contains your profile (timeline) information, you should keep it secure and take precautions when storing, sending or uploading it to any other services.

How To Download LinkedIn Contacts 1

First log into LinkedIn and click on **Connections** from the Menu Bar. You'll be taken to your connections page where you see all of the people that are connected to you.

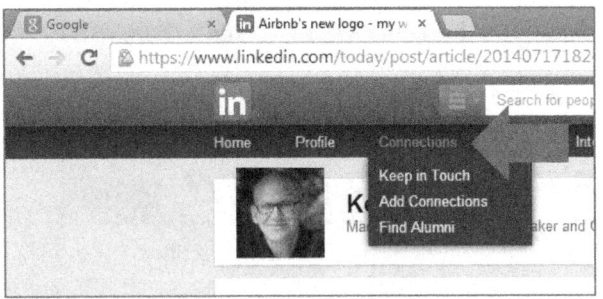

Click Settings, Choose Export Connections 2

On the extreme right hand side of the screen is a small icon that looks like a gear. This is the Settings button. Click on it to open your Settings Menu.

On the right side of that page, under Advanced Settings, you'll see a link that says "Export LinkedIn Connections". Click on that link.

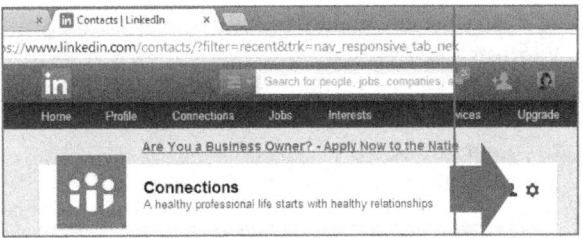

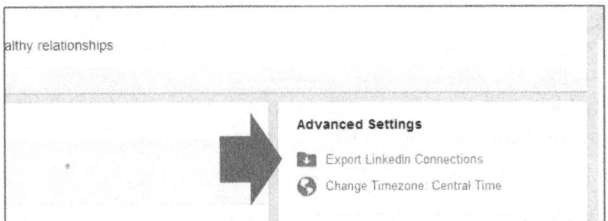

Export Them To Your Computer 3

You can use the pull-down menu to choose the format in which your contacts will be downloaded.

Most people usually use the CSV format for Windows, Excel or Outlook. You can also download your contacts in VCF format.

After you choose your format, just click the blue Export button and save the file to your computer desktop.

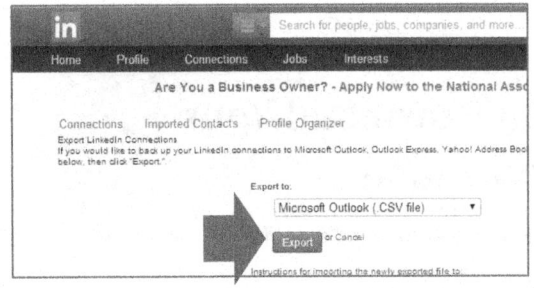

Speaking Of Outlook...

4

If you use Microsoft Outlook, don't forget that you can import these contacts directly into Outlook. Here's how you do it in Outlook 2010:

- Open Outlook and click on the **File** menu
- Choose **Open**
- Choose **Import** and then **From Another Program or File**
- For file type, choose **Comma Separated Values**
- Browse your desktop to locate the LinkedIn File you just downloaded and **Import**.

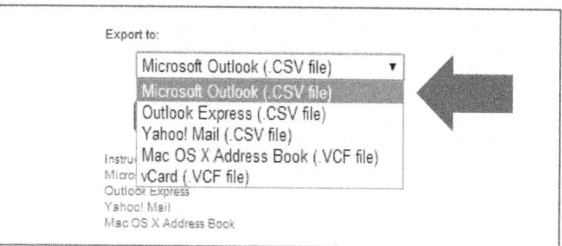

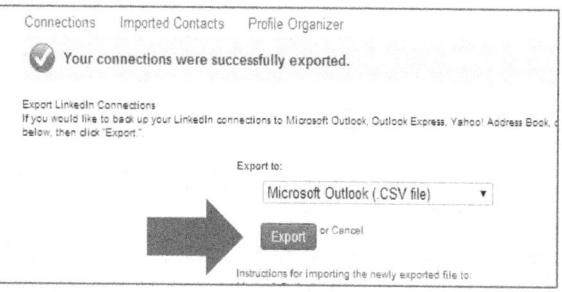

Your Business

If you're an entrepreneur, you already know what it takes to run a successful business.

You think nothing of having to wear twenty or thirty hats at once and the amount of information you have to keep in your head, especially if your business is internet-based, is astounding. But what happens if you want to enjoy your success. Let's say you want to just take off and go to Maui for two weeks. Or what if you can't run your business for a few weeks due to injury or illness?

If all of that information that you use to run your business every day is in your head, how is anyone going to step in and run things for you while you're gone? Do you have all of that information in a place where your partner or colleague can step in and seamlessly take over?

Now you do! Just open up the business life form (it's in the files you downloaded at the beginning of the book) and record all of the information that it takes to keep your business running. When you're finished, we suggest that you save and store it in at least three secure locations, including your smartphone, your password-protected iCloud or Microsoft SkyDrive account as well as **on a password-protected flash drive or portable hard drive which you'll place:**

- In a safe deposit box or water/fireproof safe in your own city.
- In a safe deposit box, water/fireproof safe, or with relatives in the city where you'll be evacuating.
- A password-protected online file repository or the file directory of your web site.
- Or take it with you on a key ring or in an emergency evacuation bin, if you ever have to evacuate your building or home office.
- You can also simply fill in the forms right in the book and toss it into waterproof/fireproof safe, locking file cabinet, safe deposit box, or at your lawyer's office. It's up to you.

Then if you, your business partner or someone acting in your behalf ever needs that information ASAP, you or they can simply retrieve it.

Just in case you finally decide to take that vacation.

Organized

The 6 Absolutely Vital Things You And Your Family Need To Put Your Life Back Together After A Major Emergency

- Enough Cash Or Access To Cash To Get Your Through 3 To 7 Days

- Documented Proof That You Own Your Home, Car And Other Property And That It Is Insured

- The Ability To Prove Your Identity To Get Assistance, Money Or Housing

- To Have The Items That Are The Most Important To You, Secure And Accessible Away From Home. These Include Vital Documents, Important Photos/Videos, Home Inventory Of Your Possessions For Insurance Purposes

- Birth, Marriage And Passports/Citizenship Certificates

- Easy Access To Your Financial Information, Bank Accounts, Safe Deposit Accounts, Direct Deposits And Investments

Social Media Accounts

I don't know about you, but we use so many passwords, user names and log on URLs for social media accounts and websites every day that it's getting harder and harder to keep track of them.

Sure you can save the URLs, user names and passwords to your browser, but what if the browser logs you out or if the website stops you in your tracks and demands that you enter your old password so that you can update your password before they'll let you into **your** account.

Or what if you need to use a different computer, tablet or phone – one that hasn't memorized your user names and passwords?

Which made us wonder something. If someone has to log on to a vital website in an emergency, what are the chances that they would remember all of the information they need to log in? Our guess? Slim to none.

That's why we created one place to store all your user names, passwords and account information. It's called My Social Life and you'll find it in the files you downloaded at the beginning of this book. Open it up, fill in your information and you can keep it on your computer, smartphone, flash drive or print it out and store it in your safe deposit box for safekeeping.

Detailing How You Want Your Social Media to be Handled

Which brings us to the last section of the My Social Life form.

Since your email, Facebook, Twitter and other accounts are an important part of your life, it only makes sense to have a say in how things are managed in your absence. And that's what the last section on the Social Life form is all about.

Now you have a place to detail exactly how you want things handled during a temporary absence, incapacity or after death. Just fill in the form, and let you spouse, business partner or significant other know where it's stored. You might even want to store a copy with your vital documents, your will and your attorney as part of your digital asset trust. Enough said.

Bank Accounts and Money

When we work on prime time television shows, the first thing the second assistant director does each week is draft a new call sheet. In case you haven't seen one, a call sheet is a list of everyone and everything necessary to produce a television show or movie. It starts with the name of each actor, and then the director, extending department by department, from the camera operators, grips and gaffers, to makeup and hair. Beside every name is their call time – the time they are expected to be on set and ready to work. The names of the regular cast and crew are pre-typed, while others, like seldom used special effects people, are handwritten.

But at the very top of the list are the names that are always there, pre-typed and in bold. The stars of the series. Without those people, there would be no show.

Whether you are running errands or evacuating for a disaster, there is one item that you always have on your list of things to bring, and it's always pre-typed and in bold.

Money.

Suppose a firefighter knocks on your door and tells you that you need to evacuate your home for at least three days. How much money would you need to take care of yourself and your family until you get back home. Five hundred dollars? A thousand? Do you have that much cash in the house?

Then what you really need is <u>access</u> to your money. Do you use a large bank or a small community bank? If it's small with branches only in your area, what if your evacuation location is in a different state? Can you take money out of an out of state ATM, without paying outrageous fees?

And what about other types of emergencies where you might need immediate access to money? A medical emergency, a car that breaks down a hundred miles away from home or federal regulators taking over your bank, severely limiting customer access for days or weeks.

Are you really prepared for anything? Let's find out.

Organized

How To Get Your Bank Accounts & Money Together

Your Mission, Should You Choose To Accept It...

... is to make sure that you can access your money when and where you need it, quickly and easily, in any situation. Start with the questions below to gauge where you are right now and then we'll show you some quick and easy steps you can take to ensure that you always have the money that you need, right at your fingertips.

1. Can you access the ATMs for your main checking or savings account outside of your own city? Can you access your money in a different state? What about across the country?

2. Do you know how much money you can take out of your primary bank's ATM at one location? During one 24 hour period? What are the fees for out of network or out of state withdrawals?

3. If there was a sudden emergency or evacuation and you could only use **cash** to provide for you and your family for an entire week how much cash would you need?

4. Do you know how much credit you have available on your credit cards? Do you know how to get an emergency increase if you need one?

5. Do you currently receive your paycheck via direct deposit, via mail or do you physically pick it up? If there was a disaster in your geographical area that affected your workplace as well as your house, would you still receive a paycheck from your company?

How Did You Do? 1

If you're like most people, you were scratching your head by the second question and running for your statements and your calculator by the third.

That's why it's always better not to put all your eggs – uh money – in one basket.

Here are a few recommendations to make sure that you can access your money, any time and any place that you need it.

Access To Your Cash 2

- Have at least one bank account that gives you nationwide access to your money. If it's not your primary account, make sure that you use the ATM card occasionally to keep it active.
- Calculate how much cash you and your family would need for a week if you had no access to your local bank.
- If you live in a disaster prone area, Consider keeping that amount of cash at home or in a safe deposit box in your evacuation location.

Your Bank Account — 3

- Place a copy of a bank statement/check from each bank account and copies of your credit cards and debit cards (front and back) on a password protected flash drive in your emergency bin, in your safe deposit box and in a safe deposit box in your evacuation location.
- If you find that you wouldn't be able to function with the limits placed on you by your current bank or credit card, consider opening up another account at a financial institution that gives you the access and services you need. You don't have to leave your old bank, but having access to what you need, when you need it is absolutely vital. After all **they're** taking care of **your** money, not the other way around.

Credit Cards — 4

- Know your credit limits and the customer service numbers you would have to call to temporarily raise them. Make sure that you note those limits, customer service numbers and any rules or guidelines on your Financial and Insurance Information Form.
- If you have two or more credit cards, make sure they are different brands. For example a Visa or a MasterCard, along with an American Express or Discover card. That way if one is not accepted at a store or restaurant, the other one probably will be.

Keeping The Money Flowing — 5

- If you haven't already, make sure that your paycheck is direct deposited into your account.
- Find out if your company has any programs or resources for employees who experience disasters/emergencies and how to take advantage of them, if you should ever need to.
- Consider creating a few more streams of income, like starting a small internet business or becoming a paid consultant, to make sure that you have additional income flowing in, in case your current employer is impacted by the same emergency you are.

Financial Information

Imagine you're out of town on a much-needed vacation. You're lounging by the sparkling pool completely relaxed because you took care of everything that needed to be done before you left the house. You even asked a neighbor to pick up your mail and overnight it to you halfway through the trip to make sure you don't get behind on any unexpected bills.

As you begin to thumb through your mail, you see a credit card statement for a card you only keep for emergencies. When you open the envelope, you're stunned to see that the card that had a zero balance when you left home, now has a $10,000 balance.

The problem is, the old statements you need to prove that you had a zero balance on the card are at home, along with card itself, the emergency customer service number you need to call and any other information that company needs, to quickly cancel the card and get those charges reversed. Impossible you say? It actually happened to someone we know. Even though their mailbox was secure, someone had stolen the convenience checks the credit card company had sent and used it to pay off her American Express card. After three straight days of phone calls to a highly suspicious credit card company, they finally got the charges off their card and the fraudulent episode out of their lives. Three days of their vacation was ruined, not to mention the level of frustration that could all have been avoided, by having the information they needed at their fingertips.

The question is, if <u>you</u> were in the same situation, would you have the information you needed accessible enough to be able to take care of the situation thousands of miles away from home?

Whether you're in the middle of a natural disaster or a man-made one, making your financial information accessible is vital. You'd BETTER be able to put your hands on every piece of your financial life in 10 minutes or less. That's called survival. And being ready to handle life's hiccups is something that every person must be able to do.

Ready? Then let's get started.

Organized

How To Get Your Financial Information Together

Your Mission, Should You Choose To Accept It...

...is to locate and gather all of the financial information you have lying around your home, safe deposit box or computer, and transfer it onto your Financial Information and Insurance Form. Then you'll place a copy of it in three different places that you, your spouse or someone acting on your behalf can access whenever necessary.

1. Your Financial Information

Grab a pencil and paper and jot down the types of financial accounts and information you currently have. This should include any Bank Accounts, CDs and Investment Accounts, IRA/401K/Retirement Accounts, Credit Cards, Mortgage Information, Rental Information, Student & Other Loans, Social Security, Pension or Retirement Benefits and financial counselors.

We'll deal with insurance and vital documents in other sections of the book.

2. Gathering All Your Financial Documents

Using the list you just compiled, **locate** and **gather** all of the information you can find for each type of financial account you, your spouse and the other adults living in your home, currently have.

3. Documenting Your Information

Grab your Financial and Insurance Form from the forms you downloaded earlier. Complete the form with all of the information you've located. Then save it or print it and put it to the side.

This information should include:

- Bank Accounts: Account Number, Branch, Type of Account, PIN, Website, Customer Service Number
- CDs and Investment Accounts: Name of Broker, Institution, Type of Account, Maturity Date, Website, Customer Service Number
- IRA/401K/Retirement Accounts: Name of Broker, Institution, Type of Account, Maturity Date, Website, Customer Service Number
- Credit Cards: Company, Account Number, Website, User Name/PIN, Customer Service Number, Credit Limit
- Mortgage Information: Company, Type, Interest Rate, Amount, Payment Address, Customer Service Number, Website, Term Length.
- Rental Information: Landlord, Rent, Date Due, Lease Term, Where You Send Payment, Landlord Contact Info.
- Student & Other Loans: Company, Type, Interest Rate, Amount, Payment Address, Customer Service Number, Website, Term Length
- Benefit Payments (i.e. Social Security or Retirement Benefits): Type of benefit, Amount, Direct Deposit/Mail, Customer Service Number, Member Number.
- Family Counselors like attorneys, brokers, financial counselors: Names, Contact Information

Which Documents Need To Be Accessible? — 4

Do you have any other information that you would need, to conduct financial business while evacuated or away from home? Will you need a copy of your bank or investment statements, loan documents or benefit award statements?

Scan all of those documents to your computer and place them in the folder you created on your desktop to hold your Backup Plan Forms and Action Plans.

Keeping Your Information Safe — 5

Place the Financial and Insurance Form inside the Backup Folder and store the folder in at least **three** secure, damage-proof locations on your computer, on your portable hard drive and safe deposit boxes. That way if one or two of the locations are inaccessible, you'll still be able to grab the information you need.

DO NOT put your or your family's social security numbers in your list of vital information, or in online files or folders, no matter how secure they are. If you have to have those numbers with you (and haven't memorized them), copy the originals and place the copies in a secure safe deposit box instead. If you need that information during an emergency or evacuation, wait to retrieve it until you can access it on your computer or portable hard drive in your secure location.

For suggestions on the best locations for your archived files and documents see "Before You Begin," at the beginning of the book.

Insurance

Unless you're purchasing a new insurance policy, the only time you think about your insurance card, policy number or the name of your agent is when you need to file a claim. That means the only time you think about your insurance information is when you're in crisis mode and least likely to remember where you put it.

The good news is, that according to our friends at State Farm, you really don't need to have that much information about your insurance policy to begin the claims process. Whether you have a small claim (golf club through the window) or a large one (a tornado just struck the entire block), all you need to have at your fingertips is the name of your insurance company, the policy number and ideally the name and phone number of your agent. Depending on your insurance agent, you might not even need that.

When we spoke with State Farm, we heard an incredible story of strength and commitment demonstrated by one agent in Joplin, Missouri. Right after the enormous tornado struck Joplin, devastating not only homes and businesses, one State Farm agent found himself without a home. He was relieved to find his office still standing, so he decided that he would just have to live in his office until he was able to find housing. Minutes after he walked in the door, his customers began walking in. Dazed and now homeless, each customer needed more care and attention than he did. They didn't even have a place to lay their heads. So the agent decided to open his office to any of his clients who needed a place to stay. In the days that followed, he began the claims process with his clients, which wasn't easy. Joplin still didn't have electricity, but between his own paperwork, his computer and his direct line to State Farm headquarters, the agent began piecing everything together, neighbor by neighbor, getting them and himself on the road to recovery.

The good news is that your Financial Information and Insurance Form is just sitting there, waiting to absorb all of your insurance information and keep it safe for you until you need it.

Go gather all of the insurance information you have for each member of your family and let's get started.

Organized

How To Get Your Insurance Information Together

Your Mission, Should You Choose To Accept It...

...is to gather all of the insurance information you currently have in the house for each member of your family and to place the information into one or more forms that are always right at your fingertips.

Calling All Insurance — 1

First grab a pencil and paper and jot down each type of insurance you and your immediate family currently have. This probably includes home owners or renters insurance, car insurance, life insurance, disability or long term health and medical.

Put aside your Medical Insurance information for now. We'll deal with that in the chapter called Medical Information.

Grab Your Flashlight, This Might Get Ugly! — 2

Using the list you just compiled, **locate** and **gather** all of the insurance cards and information you can find for each person living in your home.

Find All The Insurance Information For Each Member of Your Family Including...

- Home/Renters Insurance
- Auto/Boat
- Life/Disability

- Download and fill out one Financial Information Form containing all the policies that cover you, your spouse, your home and property

- Do a separate Financial Information Form for any member of the family who has any kind of individual insurance coverage

- Scan copies of all of the insurance cards and documents that you located

- Save or print three copies of the form you just completed, along with the documents or other materials you located & store them in at least **three** secure, damage-proof locations

Document, Document, Document — 3

Let's **document** the information that you've found.

Grab your Financial and Insurance Form from the forms you downloaded earlier in the book.

Using the information you have gathered, complete one form for all of the policies that cover you, your spouse, your home, your cars or anything else in your household. Then complete a separate form for each member of the family who has any kind of individual insurance coverage. Then save the forms to your computer, or print them out and put them to the side.

And Now For All That Paper...   4

Scan all of the insurance cards, policies and documentation that you found and place them in a special folder on your computer desktop, along with a copy of all of the Financial Information Forms you just completed.

While you're at it, if you've never done a home inventory, take a few moments to read the chapter on creating your own Home Inventory and get that taken care of right now. Then you can just toss your inventory right into the same folder. Done and done!

Keeping Your Info Secure & Nearby   5

Place the forms and scanned documents (or if you would rather, print the forms and copy the documents) and store them in at least **three** secure, damage-proof locations.

That way if one or two of the locations are inaccessible, you'll still have all the information you need at your fingertips.

Your Life

It's All About Communication

This section is very personal to us, because we found out the hard way, how vital it can be to have this part of our lives absolutely organized, armor-plated, undefeatable and secure.

We'll never forget the day we realized it wasn't.

Elaine Sullivan was an active seventy-one year old living on her own in Chicago. One day while getting ready to take a bath, she slipped and fell, striking her head and mouth on the side of the tub. Her neighbors realized they hadn't seen her all day and called the paramedics, who went in and found her, conscious, but unable to speak.

She had previously been a patient at the hospital she was taken to, she had Medicare, supplemental insurance and everything she needed. Or so we thought. Even though she was stable, injuries to her mouth made her unable to speak or swallow, so she was unable to speak for herself. Over the next few days, after a series of serious medical errors and a critical drug interaction, her condition worsened.

Elaine Sullivan was my grandma.

Despite the fact that the hospital had my mother's and my contact information for our home in Los Angeles, the hospital neglected to call us for 6 1/2 days. By the time they did, Grandma was in critical condition from a lack of the most basic care. By the time we found out she'd been hospitalized, we were unable to get to her bedside before she died, unnecessarily and alone.

As we found out, hospitals don't always make calling your next of kin their priority. Even though hospitals try to find an unconscious patient's emergency contacts and notify their families in a reasonable amount of time, they can sometimes become so busy or are so understaffed that they don't make that call as quickly as they should.

We later found that one of the main factors that caused Grandma's death was the fact that the doctors treating her didn't have her medical or prescription drug history at their fingertips. If only they had called us, we could have given them that information. Of if she had had a cell phone back then, a simple ICE Contact in her phone detailing the prescription drugs she was taking, would have absolutely saved her life.

The moral of the story is that you never know what piece of information, no matter how small, might save the life of someone you love.

So are you ready to armor-plate your family? Then let's get started.

Medical Information

There's nothing worse than having something on the tip of your tongue and not being able to remember it – **except** when the word you're trying to remember is the name of a medication that the emergency room physician needs to save your daughter's life.

As everyone knows, when a patient is brought in the emergency room unconscious, aside from obvious injuries, the doctor caring for him probably has very little information about his patient. He has no idea what he might be allergic to, what medications he's taking or the surgery he had the month before.

Emergencies can rattle the best of us and the phone number or facts you know by heart are the very ones that will elude you when you need them most!

When it comes to you and your family, it's up to **you** to fill in that missing piece BEFORE emergencies happen. And you can't leave information that important, up to your memory.

Let's get it down on paper, where it belongs!

Organized

How To Get Your Medical Information Together

Your Mission, Should You Choose To Accept It...

...is to set up a Medical History Form for each member of your family. Open the Adult and Children's Medical History Forms (you'll find them with the forms you downloaded at the beginning of the book) and let's get started.

1. What Info Am I Going To Need?

Grab a pencil and paper and jot down the types of medical information you have for each member of the family. This includes your family's medical history, medical information, names of everyone's physicians, specialists, dentists, optometrists and other health care providers and current and past prescriptions.

2. What Do You Need A Doctor To Know?

Close your eyes for a moment & imagine that you're sitting in the ER with everyone in your house. One by one, imagine that your spouse, each child or your parent has an injury, like a broken arm, or needs emergency surgery. The doctor – who doesn't know you or your family's unique medical needs – walks through the door.

What does this doctor need to know about them? Jot down all of the things that just went through your mind. Old injuries, allergies, surgeries, anything you think is important.

3. Locate & Gather All Your Information

Using those notes and the list you completed in Step 1, **locate** and **gather** all of the medical information you have at home, along with your address book or contact information for physicians and the people you'll be using for emergency contacts.

4. Create Your Family's Medical History Forms

Grab the Medical Information Form you downloaded earlier and create one for each adult and child in your family, adding all of the information you've located.

5. Choosing Your Emergency Contacts

Choose and name at least 3 emergency contacts for each person, including yourself.
- Main Emergency Contact: Include your spouse on your form and yourself on your spouse's form. For your children - you & your spouse.
- 2nd Contact: A nearby relative or good friend who you would trust enough to make informed choices on your behalf, if necessary.
- 3rd Contact: should be an out of town/out of state relative or friend.

Anything Else To Add? 6

Is there any other information you need, to deal with a medical emergency while evacuated or away from home? If so, scan or make copies of that information and place it in the same folder as your completed medical history forms.

And while you're at it, don't forget to put ICE (In Case Of Emergency) Contacts in your and your family's smartphones along with a copy or link to your medical history forms. That way if you ever need quick access to a family member's medical history you'll have it right at your fingertips. Need instructions on ICE Contacts? Just go to that section of the book.

Now For Safekeeping... 7

Print, scan or make three copies of the form you just completed, along with the documents or other materials you need to have grabbable, and store them in at least **three** secure, damage-proof locations. That way if one or two of the locations are inaccessible, you'll still be able to grab the information you need.

You should also consider attaching the forms to your emergency contact cards (school & work) as well as placing a set on a secure web server and putting a link to them in your smartphone, so you'll always have your medical history forms at your fingertips wherever you are.

How To Put An ICE Contact On Your Phone

Did you know that your smartphone can save your life?

And it's not just Androids and iPhones but any kind of cell phone.

The secret is letting your phone do the talking for you in an emergency. And the way to do that, is with ICE.

What is ICE?

During Hurricane Katrina and the London bombings, so many people were injured, unconscious and separated from their families that a British paramedic, Bob Brotchie came up with the idea of putting ICE Contacts (In Case Of Emergency) on cell phones. Now, when a patient who is unconscious or unable to speak comes into the emergency room, hospitals worldwide check patient's smartphones for an ICE contact, to help them locate their next of kin.

Everyone in your family should have an ICE contact in his or her smartphone. In fact, they should actually have two just in case the first contact is unavailable. And even if you already have an ICE Contact, that doesn't mean that it has everything in it that it should, to save your life or the life of your spouse or your children.

If you already have an ICE Contact on your phone, don't just skip this section. Take a look at shortcut sheet to make sure your contact has everything it should, before using the instructions to ICE all the other phones in your household.

Grab your phones and let's get started.

Organized

How To Set Up An iCE Contact On Your iPhone

What Is ICE?

During Hurricane Katrina, so many people were injured & separated from their families, that emergency workers came up with the idea of putting an ICE – In Case Of Emergency – contact in their cell phones. Now, hospitals worldwide, check patient's phones for their ICE contact, to locate their next of kin.

Everyone in your family should have 2 ICE contacts on his cell phone, just in case the first person is unavailable. So let's learn how to set up your ICE contact on your iPhone.

Grab Your Phone & Let's Get Started — 1

Who will your two ICE Contacts be? Your spouse, partner, best friend, parent or close relative?

Once you decide, **Touch** the **Contacts Icon** on your iPhone to open up your Contacts. Click on the plus sign **+** to add a new contact and **touch the Name Field**. Don't put the name of your contact in this field, only the word **ICE**.

Now touch the **Company Name Field**. This is where you put your contact's name and relationship to you. For example, John Jones - Husband.

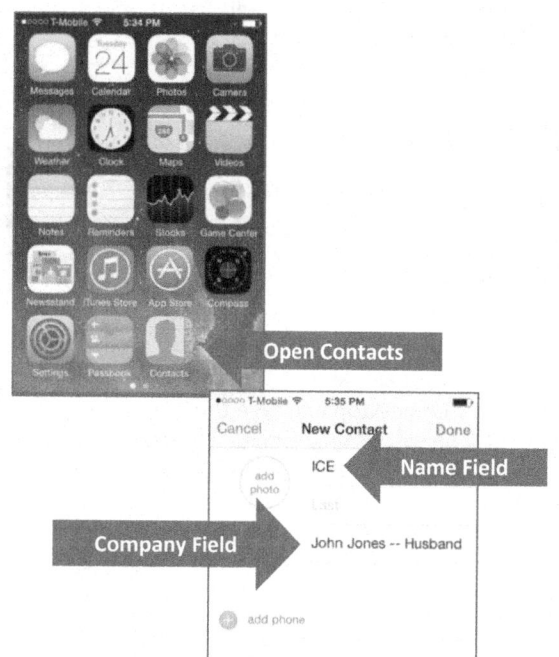

Enter All of Your Information — 2

Put **all the information you possibly can** into your two ICE Contacts. For example:
- Your emergency contact's Main Number/Cell number/ Work number
- Email Address & IM, Twitter and Facebook address (in case landlines are down & you need to send an emergency message)
- Other info, for example, days that the contact is at a certain location
- Add extra fields if you need them.
- Use the Notes Section to list your Allergies, Current Medications or the Names & Numbers of your Physicians.

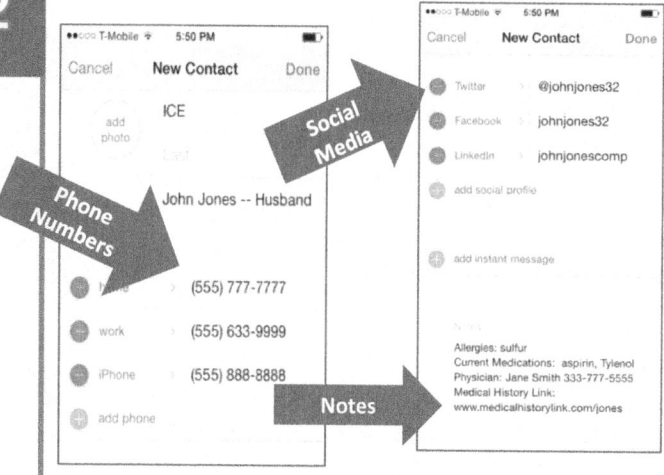

What About Your Medical History? | 3

Need more than just a few lines to communicate your medical history? Then create a medical history form and store it to a password protected online folder & place a link to the form in your ICE contact. This way a doctor can access your, your spouse's or your kids basic medical history, while you're en route to the hospital. You'll find Adult and Children's Medical History Forms inside the Backup Plan Forms you downloaded at the beginning of the book and instructions in the Medical Information chapter of this book.

To add fields to your contact, press the field name until the menu appears, then choose the field or label you want.

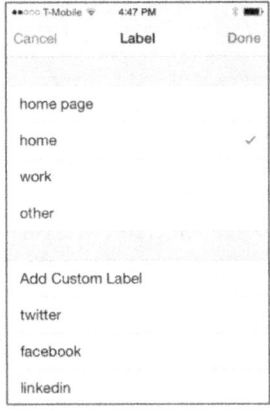

Make Your ICE Contacts Stand Out | 4

Make your ICE contacts stand out, by using the **Add Photo** function to upload a graphic to your phone, like the ones on this page. You'll find them with the Backup Plan Forms you downloaded at the beginning of the book. Just save them to your desktop and save the graphic to the photos on your phone. **Touch Edit**, **Choose** the picture & **Save** it to your contact.

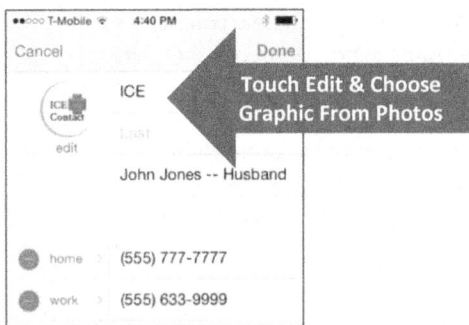

Is Your Phone Password Protected? | 5

THAT's why we had you put nothing but the word ICE in the Name field of your ICE Contact. Even when your iPhone is password locked, all an Emergency Room has to do is **Press and Hold Down** the **Main Home Key** on your phone to access Siri. Then say to Siri, "**Contacts ICE**". Siri will then display all the information you have saved as ICE. This won't work on some iPhones. It depends on the model and operating system.

To test your phone, set up your ICE contact, lock your iPhone and ask Siri to locate the contact. If it doesn't work, simply put your ICE Contact information on your lock screen as a graphic. Problem solved!

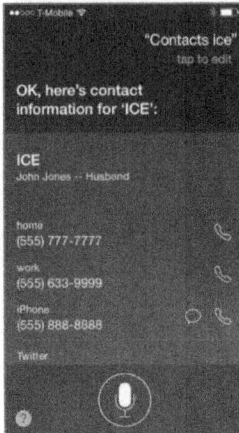
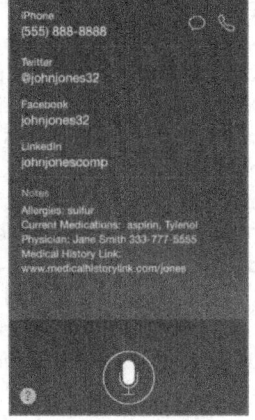

Your Own Mobile Command Center

6

While you're at it, you can even **turn your phone** into a **Mobile Command Center**. Just store copies of your family's medical history forms, emergency action plans, checklists and Evacuation Plan Form (in your downloads), right on your phone and those of each member of your immediate family.

And while you have them, don't forget to put ICE Contacts on their phones as well, including along with each other's contact information. That way you can all get in touch with each other quickly in an emergency.

Completed Contact →

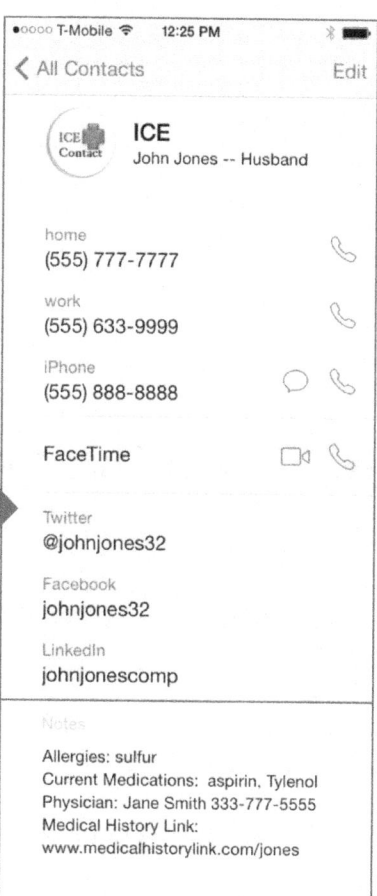

How To Fill Out Your Family's Emergency Contact Cards

In the days after 9/11, 2,100 children were left stranded in daycare.

Why?

Because their parents neglected to fill out one field on their emergency contact cards.

> "Who should we contact if you are not able to pick up your child?"

How could something so basic, strand two thousand children on one of the scariest days in American history?

Fear.

The inability or refusal to take two minutes to think through what might happen, if they and their spouse were unable to reach their child. The ridiculous thing is, it doesn't even have to take a real emergency for this to happen. You could be stuck on the freeway, or trapped in an airplane you were certain would arrive on time.

So take a few moments to think about it. And please, please don't just jot down the first name that pops into your head!

Imagine that you have an accident or are in the middle of a transportation nightmare and you and your spouse are unable to pick up your child from school one afternoon. Now imagine that you can't get to her for two or three days. Who would you want taking care of her?

Choosing Your Emergency Contacts

You need someone who knows your child extremely well. Someone who would be able to calm her down and would have the energy to care for her. Someone who knows what she likes and dislikes. And, in case of extreme emergency like September 11th, it would really help to have someone with the ability, brains and fortitude to help locate you or your spouse, if overburdened emergency personnel weren't able to help.

That's the kind of thought you need to put into emergency planning, especially where your children are concerned.

Medical History

Now what about your child's medical history? Some schools or day care centers don't even provide a card for medical history, or the one they provide might be so sparse that it would be useless in a true medical emergency. Don't forget that you can simply create your own medical history card and see that it's stored with your child's records. That way you can be sure that the information you would want emergency personnel to have in an emergency, will be right at their fingertips.

If you have already completed the section on Medical Information, you already have Medical History Forms for you and your children. So grab their forms and let's see how you did with them.

Did you include a current list of chronic conditions, allergies, medications and vitamins along with the dosage? A list of all of your child's health providers including specialists, dentists and other professionals who see your child on a regular basis?

Did you jot down things that a nurse or physician might need to know to help calm your child down while treating her, until you're able to be at the hospital? Your child's likes and dislikes, favorite foods or toys or anything else that might help. No matter how old your child is, kids tend to regress a bit when they're hurting or frightened, so the information you provide here can go a long way towards keeping them calm and helping the medical team give them the treatment they need until you arrive at the hospital.

Take the emergency contact card from your child's school or daycare provider and fill it in with your carefully-chosen emergency contacts as well as the information from the medical information form. Like we said, if there's not enough room to detail important information, just ask the school to store the medical information form you created earlier along with the emergency card. And be sure to store the medical information form, or a link to it, in your smartphone in case you need to refer to it in an emergency.

Your Own Emergency Contact Card

Just because you and your spouse are adults doesn't mean that you don't need to take your own emergency cards seriously. Do we have to remind you about all the runners who have been rushed to the hospital in the middle of a 10K without a scrap of medical information? Didn't think so!

The moment you begin a job, register for school or run a marathon, you're going to have to fill out your own card. The best way to do it? Exactly like you did for your kids.

Before you jot down your spouse and no one else as an emergency contact, take some time to think of another person or two, who you would want to be notified in an emergency. Your spouse might be out of town, stuck with a dead cell phone or worse might be involved in the same emergency.

If that's the case who would you want to be there with you? Who would you trust to make decisions for you? To take care of your children if need be, or keep things going until your spouse or other relatives arrive?

And take the same care with your medical history as you did with your children's. If there isn't enough room on the contact form for allergies, medications or other vital information, attach the medical information form you created earlier, or if you're not comfortable with that, attach an additional page of information to make sure your emergency form would actually help in an emergency!

Taking five minutes now to turn your emergency contact card into a truly valuable document, could be one of the smartest things you've ever done.

Your Emergency Wallet Cards

Think about your daily routine for a moment. Do you always take your phone and your wallet, purse or backpack with you when you go out? Or do you go running wearing nothing but a top, shorts, sneakers and an iPod? What about your spouse? Does he or she always carry a wallet and a phone, or almost never?

Do any of these "walletless" or "phoneless" situations sound familiar?
- The guy running out for a second with nothing but a few bucks to get a quart of milk.
- People out jogging, carrying nothing but some water and an iPod.
- The Alzheimer's patient who slips away from his caregiver and wanders down the street.
- The parents running out the door to pick up the kids, leaving their driver's license and other ID behind.
- The high-school or college students who don't "need" their student ID card to go out partying.

If you and your family don't have the information you need **with you w**hen you need it, all the emergency planning and information gathering you've done will do you absolutely no good!

Not to worry. We've got you covered – with GET YOUR STUFF TOGETHER's Emergency Wallet Cards. By the way, you can find them in the forms you downloaded at the beginning of this book. Just open them up on your computer, fill them out and print them, or print them out and fill them in by hand. You can even laminate them if you want. Just be sure to create a card for every member of your immediate family.

Okay but what about those walletless situations? How will the wallet cards help me if I'm not carrying a wallet?

It's simple. Print out extra copies of the emergency wallet cards you'll be making and tuck them into the clothing or items that you take with you on your short jaunts.

Here's how to do it.

Organized

How To Create Your Family's Emergency Wallet Cards

Your Mission, Should You Choose To Accept It...

...is to create an Emergency Wallet Card for each member of your family. These are great for situations when your you don't have a cell phone or regular wallet with you. Just slip them into a pocket, iPod, Shoewallet – any place.

1. Open The Wallet Card Document

Open up the Emergency Wallet Card from the forms and plans you downloaded at the beginning of the book. If you've been working through the other sections in the book, use the information and contacts you have gathered and Family Emergency/Evacuation Plans you have created to fill in a card for each member of your family.

The first side includes the person's name, birth year/blood type, physician and emergency contact names/numbers, allergies and if you want, a link to their medical information form. On the reverse are the details of your family's emergency plan.

2. Printing Out Your Wallet Cards

Once the cards are complete, print out wallet cards for each member of your family.

For the first set, print them out on thick cardstock – you can even laminate them – and place each one into a plastic lanyard (around the neck) card holder or a Shoewallet, and put them into your Plastic Evacuation Bin. Placing the wallet card into a card holder will not only keep it safe and dry, but will make it easy to locate and during an evacuation.

3. Where Else Can I Put Them?

Then print out two or three additional wallet cards for each person and place them in:
- Their regular wallets,
- Their work or school ID badges and
- Inside their Smartphone case
- One of several products, including our personal favorite the Shoewallet, that are tailor-made to hold your emergency wallet cards, along with your driver's license, credit cards, key and even a few dollars anytime you leave the house or the office without a purse or wallet. We happen to like Shoewallet because it securely fastens to your shoes, a belt loop, backpack or pocket.

When you stash emergency cards in different places, each member of your family will have a way to keep their emergency information and emergency plan available at all times, no matter where they are or what they're doing.

4. What About The Kids?

Since children don't carry wallets or driver's licenses, make sure that they have ID cards with current emergency contact information in a few different locations, like in a backpack, an inside jacket pocket, in a Shoewallet on their sneakers or tucked into the back of a cell phone or iPod.

Family Evacuation Plan

If you and your family had to evacuate your home because of a tornado, an earthquake or wildfire, where would you go?

There's a lot to consider. "Location A is close enough to home to check on the house if we had to, but what if the entire city is affected? Then again, if we go to Location B, how will I ever get to work?"

Is your head hurting yet?

Not to worry. A – That's exactly why we want you to go through this exercise now and not when a firefighter is knocking at the door. And B – That's also why we suggest that you choose three locations and if an emergency ever rears its ugly head, opt for the one that fits your needs.

A great Evacuation Plan has two objectives:
1. To figure out the best location for your evacuation.
2. To help you gather your family and get you safely to your location with everything you need once you get there.

In other words…

Without A Plan

You run to the bank after a disaster strikes to grab copies of your birth certificate and the deed to your house out of your safe deposit box.

The bank is closed.

And under 10 feet of water.

With A Plan

You drive right past the bank and fifty miles later, arrive at your planned evacuation location where a box of your important papers and a flash drive full of your family photos are waiting for you.

Along with an extra ATM card. Fresh clothes. And a Starbucks card.

First we'll walk you through choosing your locations and sketching out a plan. Then once the plans are set, put the details on your family's emergency wallet cards. If you want, you can also give a card to the person you chose to be your out-of-area contact.

Let's get started.

Organized

How To Create Your Family Evacuation Plan

Your Mission, Should You Choose To Accept It...

...is to choose an evacuation location and plan for you and your family to use, if you ever have to unexpectedly evacuate your home or your area. No matter what the reason, you're going to have to know where you're going, before you can get there. Here's how to do it.

Where Will We Go? 1

We recommend that you choose three different locations, because that will give you and your family a variety of choices that will keep you safe, no matter what circumstances you might face.

- One location should be near your neighborhood, to be used in an emergency that only impacts your home.
- One location should be out of your immediate area but in the same state. This is for a regional emergency.
- One location should be out of state, for situations with widespread danger, like a wildfire or an earthquake.

Choose Three Locations

- Near Home
- Same State
- Another State

That Have These Qualities

- The locations have the stores or services your family might need like doctors and banks
- You and your family can easily commute to your jobs or work from home
- The locations have the furniture and supplies that you and your family would need for two or three weeks or longer

Keep In Mind

- The needs of the family members traveling with you
- How you'll get there (car, bus, airplane)
- Any pets that will be travelling with you

Choose A Great Evacuation Location 2

Before you try to zero in on a perfect location, come up with as many different locations as you can that you and your family would be able to use for evacuation.

As you consider each location, think about:
- The needs of the people traveling with you
- How you'll get there (car, bus, plane)
- Any pets that will be traveling with you

Does It Have What You Need? 3

Once you're pretty certain you have the right places, consider whether this location has what you and your family would actually need.

For instance if would need to stay in that location for two or three weeks, would it be close enough to the stores or services your family might need, like pharmacies, clothing, banks and doctors?

Would you be able to get to work from that location, or are you able to work from home?

Does it have the furniture and supplies necessary for two or three weeks?

The Staging Area 5

Now that you've chosen your locations, choose two places for you and your family to gather during an emergency, so that you can travel to your evacuation location together. One place should be near your home or work and the other farther from your home in case your area is completely inaccessible.

Put the addresses and phone numbers of these two meeting places on your family's emergency cards.

We Have A Winner! 4

No location is perfect, so if you came up with one or two things your location would be lacking, be sure to note them on your Family Evacuation Plan, so that you can take care of it before you get there.

Appoint An Out Of Town Contact 6

It's also a good idea to appoint an out of town contact to help you while your family deals with the aftermath of an emergency.

Even though you might not be able to call people right in your own area after an emergency, you can often call long distance. A distant friend can be a touch point for the entire family until communication is restored.

Once you choose an out of town relative or friend as a contact, check with them to make sure that they're willing to help. If so, give them a copy of your emergency plan and wallet card, so they'll be able to help, if the need ever arises.

Creating Your Plan 7

Open the Family Evacuation Plan (you'll find it inside the Backup Plan Forms you downloaded at the beginning of the book). Here are a few questions to answer before you draft your plan:
- Who Is Evacuating With You?
- Who Will Do What?
- Temporary Housing
- Transportation Plans/Travel Information
- Pet Information
- Out of State and Local Contacts
- Contact Information For Everyone Who Will Be Evacuating With You As Well As Your Out of Town Contact.

Evacuation Checklist

In the last section, you decided where you and your family would go during an evacuation and how you were going to get there. So now that's decided, what do you need to take with you?

Money? ID? Clothes?

And before you know it, you're running off in 10 different directions at once, dumping anything you can think of on the couch.

We know. We've been there.

So let's go back to our original question. A firefighter knocks on your door. You now have ten minutes to get everything you, your spouse and your two kids will need to get through the next three days without setting foot back in your house.

What do you need to take? Simple. Everything on your Evacuation Checklist.

Your checklist will include everything that you and the people traveling with you can't do without and can't easily replace while away from home, like contact lenses or an extra set of car keys. It will also include the things you need to do or remember before locking up the house (including locking up the house) along with the names of the people responsible for each item or task.

For the next few days, pay attention to the things you and your family regularly use. If you identify other items that you can't do without, simply add them to the checklist.

Are you ready to create your checklist? Then let's get started.

Organized

How To Create Your Evacuation Checklist

Your Mission, Should You Choose To Accept It...

...is to create an Evacuation Checklist that will detail all the things that you would have to do, take and remember in case you ever have to evacuate your home in an emergency.

Before We Get Started... 1

If you haven't already created your Family Evacuation Plan, please go to that section and complete it before tackling this checklist.

Open The Evacuation Checklist... 2

You'll find your Evacuation Checklist form in the files you downloaded at the beginning of this book.

In Section One, you'll list all of things you need to do before you leave the house. For example, turning off the water or unplugging appliances -- anything you would normally do before or after a disaster.

What Will You Put On Your List? 3

In Section Two, list all the items that you will be taking with you, its location and the person responsible for grabbing it. Include everything that you and the people traveling with you can't do without and can't easily replace.

Here are a few things to get you started:
- **First aid supplies**
- **Non-Perishable Food, Diapers, infant formula**
- **Cash**
- **Toys/things to keep children occupied**
- **Flash drive/portable hard drive containing vital documents**
- **House/Car Keys**
- **Flashlight, Batteries, Can Opener**
- **Journals, diaries, letters**
- **ID and Wallet Cards for everyone traveling, Insurance/Medicare cards**
- **Cell phone, Battery operated radio**
- **Toiletries**
- **Tools, gloves, Dust Mask, Whistle/Flares**
- **Comfortable, weather-appropriate clothing**

Keepsakes 4

In Section Three, list all the keepsakes you need to take with you and note where they are located. This includes photo albums/family histories, journals, diaries, a few favorite pieces of clothing and cherished books.

Location, Location, Location 5

Take a few moments to picture the location where you'll stay while evacuated.
- Is there anything that the location doesn't have that you'll need when you get there?
- Is there anything currently on your checklist to take, that is already in that location? If so, take it off your list.
- If you'll be evacuating to the home of a relative or a friend, consider leaving a box of emergency items with them the next time you visit. The less you need to take, the more quickly you can evacuate.

What If You Stay Home? 6

In Section Four, list any emergency supplies that you will need if you choose to remain in your home during an emergency, like a storm or after an earthquake.

For ideas and instructions on what you might need, see our blog post How To Earthquake Proof Your Bedroom at http://rnn10.wordpress.com

Keeping Your List At Your Fingertips 7

Print, scan or make three copies of the Checklist you just completed, and store them in at least **three** secure, damage-proof locations. That way if one or two of the locations are inaccessible, you'll still be able to grab the information you need.

If your Checklist is **on paper, you can place it:**
- In your watertight Plastic Evacuation Bin.
- In one other waterproof, easy to reach location in your home or office.

If your Checklist is **on computer, you can place it:**
- On your smartphone, as well as an iPad or laptop computer – whatever you would have at your fingertips or take with you during evacuation.
- If your phone is unable to store documents, upload the checklist to your password-protected online file repository or even the file directory of your family's personal web site. This way if you need a copy of your information or forms quickly, you can retrieve them from any Internet-enabled computer.

Get Back To Life Plan

Scenario One

Imagine that a hurricane strikes your area. You and your family are in your evacuation location two days after the hurricane subsides. The phone rings. It's a friend of yours calling to tell you that your home is badly damaged, and doubts that you will be able to live in it for at least a month or two. After you and your family get past the initial shock, you finally feel strong enough to open your Backup Plan Notebook. There you find your Get Back To Life Plan and begin making calls to your insurance agent, your contractor and your boss. You call the local real estate agent in your evacuation city and ask her to begin looking for temporary housing, register your children in the local school and begin calling the contacts on your list to help you settle in.

Getting settled is easier than you thought since you have copies of all of the vital documents you need, like your birth certificates and property deeds in a safe deposit box at the local bank. With a little hard work and a lot of courage, you and your family are back to living a normal life in a matter of weeks.

Scenario Two

Imagine that a hurricane strikes your area. You and your family are in your evacuation location two days after the hurricane subsides. The phone rings. It's a friend of yours calling to tell you that your home is badly damaged, and doubts that you will be able to live in it for at least a month or two. After you and your family get past the initial shock, you realize that you have no idea what you're going to do.

Same scenario, same challenges, **one difference**.

One path comes with a **plan** for finding your way back.

Facing a disaster without giving yourself a plan to recover from it is like trying to build a house with no blueprint and no tools! So let's get started on that blueprint.

Organized

How To Create Your Get Back To Life Plan

Your Mission, Should You Choose To Accept It...

Facing a disaster without giving yourself a plan to recover from it; is like trying to build a house with no blueprint and no tools! So your mission today is to create a Get Back To Life Plan that's ready to help you and your family recover from any disaster or life interrupting event. This Shortcut Sheet has only two steps. First answer the 12 questions below. Then, open the Get Back To Life Plan (you'll find it inside the Backup Plan Forms you downloaded at the beginning of the book) and fill in the blanks. By the way, if you haven't chosen your evacuation location yet, go to that chapter and complete that exercise first.

1. Think about your evacuation location. Does it have all the furniture and supplies we will need for up to one month?

2. What type of clothing would we need?

3. Can we store any basic supplies there before they're needed, or do we need to purchase supplies when we arrive?

4. How will we handle our bank accounts, paying our monthly bills? How much emergency cash do we need to have while traveling? What are our credit card limits and toll free numbers for emergency increases?

5. How will we work? Will I be able to receive my paycheck in that location? Will we work remotely or have to look for new positions? What people or contacts can we call about temporary or permanent jobs?

6. How will we handle our medical, dental and prescription medicine needs while in the new location? Can we get referrals to doctors and dentists that we can use, if need be, when we get there?

7. How long can we stay in our evacuation location? If the evacuation lasts longer than we think, where will we go/stay? Do we have real estate contacts if we need to find new permanent or temporary housing?

8. How will we secure the property or vehicles we have to leave behind?

| 9 | How will we take care of our pets during the evacuation and until we find new permanent housing? |

| 10 | How will we handle our transportation needs? What contacts will we need to purchase or lease vehicles? |

| 11 | How will we handle our daycare needs? How will we handle getting our children into school if it becomes necessary? What documents will we need to enroll them in a new school in a temporary or new location? |

| 12 | How will we handle any special needs in our family? How will we handle any potential problems we have identified? |

Before You Begin Creating Your Plan... 1

Before you start filling in the details of the plan, take a moment to read through the questions on the Shortcut Sheet first and think about your responses, keeping the needs of your family in mind. If necessary, go over them with your spouse or other family members. Once you're certain of the answers, go ahead and fill in Section One.

Your Contacts 3

In the final section, write down the contact information for your real estate agents, financial contacts, job/career information, schools, doctors and any other professionals or information that you might need to establish yourself in the new city temporarily or permanently.

Taking It Step By Step 2

Using those answers, grab a sheet of paper and step by step, outline what you and your family will do during the evacuation. For example: During our evacuation we will stay in X location. I will be working remotely with my company laptop and our pets will be staying with Aunt Mary. We will take care of our finances in this way...

Fill in as many details as you can, so that you'll have a clear picture of where and how you will live while you're away from home. When it's finished, type it into the Get Back to Life Plan.

And When You're Finished... 4

Once you're finished, print, scan or make three copies of the Plan, and store it in at least **three** secure, damage-proof locations, including a password-protected online file repository. This way if you need a copy of your information or forms quickly, you can retrieve them from any Internet-enabled computer.

And while you're at it, store a copy in your and your family's smartphones as well, so that you can all instantly access and use the plan whenever you need it, even if an emergency occurs while you're away from home.

How To Make Your Family Findable

Living In A State of Constant Communication

In the middle of a busy, but quiet day in a Midwestern university lecture hall, the silence was pierced by a sudden hail of gunfire. Students ran out of the hall and ducked under tables. Those who couldn't move tried to make themselves as invisible as possible until help arrived. That day at Northern Illinois University, five students lost their lives. Many others were injured.

As the police and security were struggling to control the situation, a number of the student's parents not only knew that their children were all right, but they knew exactly what was happening in real time.

So how did some people have a window into the NIU tragedy while others did not? Facebook and Twitter! As unlikely as it sounds, students ingeniously found a way to use their favorite method of keeping in touch with friends, as a tool to connect to the outside world in the middle of a crisis.

Students caught under desks and tables grabbed their smartphones and started communicating. Tweets went out on Twitter, notes and messages went up on Facebook pages, telling friends and family that students, who were literally in the thick of things, were all right.

Others told loved ones or security officers the location of trapped students, facilitating their rescue. Friends started texting each other to find out where everyone was and, in the hours that followed, created Facebook pages memorializing the fallen.

It was an amazing display of people, who are connected 24/7, using that same technology to communicate, connect, survive and heal.

During the Japan earthquake cell phone towers barely worked because of earthquake damage and overloaded networks. But Wi-Fi was up and running. So what kept the Japanese connected with their families and the outside world? Twitter, Facebook, Skype and YouTube!

Smartphones, tablets and notebook computers are a phenomenal way to stay in touch during an emergency. Whether you send an email, text, tweet or Facebook message, you can find out the location and condition of everyone you love in seconds. In a dire emergency, you can even send help, confirm or update emergency plans and even mobilize family and friends to be at the side of the ill or injured, using real time information.

Since disasters are completely unpredictable, the only way to prepare yourself and your family is to give yourselves as many different avenues of communication as possible. You never know which one will make the difference.

Want to learn how your family can use technology to communicate during an emergency? Then let's get started.

Organized

How To Make Your Family Findable

Your Mission, Should You Choose To Accept It...

...is to learn how your family can use technology to communicate during an emergency, then create a smartphone based communication plan to use the next time you have to gather everybody in a hurry.

1. Updating Your Smartphones

When you created your Family Evacuation Plan (if you haven't done that yet, go do it now – we'll wait for you), you listed the phone numbers, email addresses and social media addresses for each family member in your household.

Now we're going to take that one step further by adding all of that information to each family member's smartphones. While you're at it, add new contacts on everyone's phones for all of your out-of-area emergency contacts as well.

3. When Time Is An Issue

Using a social media platform like HootSuite.com may help. With HootSuite, you can send a single message that can be posted to Twitter, Facebook and LinkedIn simultaneously, ensuring that your family or friends would see your message immediately, no matter what site they happen to be on at the moment.

2. Direct Messaging

If cell phone service is down and you are unable to text, don't forget that Twitter and Facebook can also be used to send direct messages - personal messages that go only to the recipient. Here's a quick tutorial.

First, you need to make sure that every member of your family is following or has "liked" all of the other family members on Twitter and Facebook, so you can direct message each other.

- For Twitter, click on Messages, then Direct Messages and then type in @ and the family member's username. Then type in your message and hit send.
- For Facebook, click the little message icon at the top of your page (between the little people and the little earth). Then click Send New Message and type in the name of the recipient or recipients and click send.

4. The Value Of A Photo

During the Joplin tornado, even lifelong residents found themselves disoriented when the tornado turned their normal landmarks into kindling. If your spouse or kids don't know where they are after an emergency and need help a quick photo texted or uploaded to Instagram or Facebook could help you locate them. This is especially true of GPS enabled phones or photos with geo-location.

Creating A Communications Plan — 5

Once you and your family have updated your phones and completed your evacuation plans, sit down with them to discuss the ways you can use technology to stay in touch with each other during a disaster.

Come up with some sample scenarios; for example, if a disaster were to happen while your family members were at work, at school or running errands during a normal day.
- How would you connect with each other?
- Would you text each other, or would calling or emailing be faster?
- If you have teens or young adults at home, their natural proclivity may be to send out a text or a tweet on Twitter, to update everyone, including you, on their location or situation.
- Find out the types of communication everyone prefers and then create an emergency communication plan that makes sense for your family.

Grab The Sat Phone! — 7

If you're in an area with frequent emergencies like tornadoes or hurricanes, live out in the country or have a family member in a foreign country, consider getting satellite phones.

They work in remote areas where there is no cell phone coverage and when cell towers are down. If you don't want the expense of a dedicated satellite phone, there are a few devices like Spot Connect Satellite (www.findmespot.com) that turn your smartphone into a satellite phone.

What If... — 6

Another great discussion to have with your family, especially with school age children, is what they would do if they had to get a hold of you but the cell phone system was out, or what to do if there was an area-wide blackout. Don't laugh, that actually happed to us in California!

Kids are so used to technology that they might not have the experience that they need to do things the old school way. The best way to plan is to give yourselves as many ways as possible to stay connected. Then if one or two normal methods are unusable, you'll all simply turn to a different method to reach each other.

Code Word Clearance Or Higher — 8

Consider creating a Family Emergency Code or Code Word. This is a code or word that only you and your immediate family know. When a family member says it, texts it or emails it to the rest of the family, it signals that they're in trouble and need help.

It's only to be used in extreme emergency and means that everyone needs to drop what they're doing and establish contact with each other, immediately.

Find My Family ASAP! — 9

Find My Friends is an iPhone app that is designed to let you know at a glance where your friends are. But you can also use it to immediately locate your children, spouse and loved ones in an emergency.
All your family has to do is allow you access on their phones, and if need be, you can immediately see where everyone is in real time, complete with map and directions.

Mobile Command Center

What if I told you there was one thing that you own and probably have with you right now, that can give you the support, the information and ability you need to keep everyone and everything you love safe and sound, PLUS the power to gather your family in seconds no matter where they are? What is it?

It's your smartphone.

You've done all the work – all your Backup Plan Forms and Action Plans are sitting in their folder on your hard drive and you've used the Shortcuts to save and store all of your data and keepsakes. All that's left is making it accessible. And the best way to do that is to use the tool that you always have with you.

Our goal for this section is simple.

If you had to face a major emergency minutes from now and the <u>only</u> thing you had with you was your smartphone, you should be able to:
- Call or communicate with all the people you love within 10 minutes.
- Communicate your basic medical information and your emergency contacts to emergency personnel even if you are injured and unable to speak for yourself.
- Keep yourself and your family up and running using only the information in your phone until you reach home or your pre-planned evacuation location.
- Access all of the emergency forms and plans you created and all of the data, photos, videos, movies and other items you saved and stored while working through this book.

If you would also like to have a hard copy of your emergency plans to refer to as well, grab a sturdy three-ring notebook and print out a copy of each of your Action Plans along with any other information that you want to include. Make sure that form or plan has its own tab, so that you can easily find or replace outdated pages. We suggest using a ring binder that has a hard, washable, vinyl cover and pockets to catch papers, maps or any other items that can easily become lost.

Your ICE Contacts

If you haven't already finished putting ICE Contacts on your phone and the rest of the family's phones, do it now. Make sure that your contact and your spouse's contact contains links to every other family member's medical information sheet.

The Rest Of The Family
When you created your Family Evacuation Plan, you detailed each family member's email addresses, text, user names and cell numbers on the plan. Now it's time to take that one step further by making sure each member of your family's smartphones have:

- Every other family member's complete contact information, including all social media handles and work/school schedules.
- Full contact information for each Out Of Area Contact.
- A copy of your Family Evacuation Plan.
- The addresses and phone numbers of these two meeting places highlighted in their Contacts.
- An extra copy of their emergency wallet cards.

Are you ready to pull it all together? Here's how to turn your smartphone into your very own Mobile Command Center.

Organized

How To Turn Your Phone Into A Mobile Command Center

Your Mission, Should You Choose To Accept It...

...is to take all the material you created and archived in the book and to make it accessible wherever you are, whenever you need it.

First, here's a quick rundown of the material we've created or archived in the book. Each form, plan or keepsake will either be placed in your smartphone, or be accessible to you from your smartphone.

Here is how we've broken down each type of information.

1. You'll Need These Actual Forms, Plans & Information

Family's Medical Information
Family Evacuation Plan
Evacuation Checklist
Evacuation Quicklist
Get Back To Life Plan
Your ID/Emergency Wallet Cards
My Social Life
Business Information
Emergency Contact Information (should already be in phone)
Family Member's Contact Information (should already be in phone)

2. You'll Need Access To This Archived Data

Scans of Print Photos
Digital Photos
Home Videos/Home Movies
Data
Music
Family Recipes
Family History
Voice Mails or Special Recordings
Contacts and Address Books
LinkedIn/Facebook Contacts

3. You'll Need Access To These Forms & Plans

Home Inventory
Vital Documents
Financial Information
Insurance

Need Actual Forms & Plans — 1

These forms and plans are crucial for emergencies large and small, so you should definitely keep them at your fingertips – or in this case, right on your smartphone. Unless you have Microsoft Word software on your phone, save each of them as PDFs and place them on Dropbox or iCloud or other online file service so that you can open and read them right on your phone.

You may also want to save them directly onto your phone or tablet so that they will be available if your cell phone or Wi-Fi service is down. There are a couple of ways to do this. If you can find the directions on how to save a PDF onto your smartphone from the phone's manufacturer, just follow those directions. Or a quicker way would be to convert the PDFs to ePub files and save them to iBooks or Google Books for quick access. (see http://www.pdfmate.com/read-pdf-on-ipad-iphone-ipod.html for a tutorial).

Need Access To These Forms & Plans — 2

These forms may contain some sensitive information, so instead of saving them directly onto your phone, place them on a secure password protected server or password protected Cloud-based server, like Dropbox, iCloud or Sky Drive and place the link to those folders in a special contact on your smartphone. Do not store the password with the link.

One important note: DO NOT put your or your family's social security numbers in your list of vital information, or in online files or folders, no matter how secure they are. If you have to have those numbers with you (and haven't memorized them), copy the originals and place the copies in a secure safe deposit box instead. If you need that information during an emergency or evacuation, wait to retrieve it until you can access it on your computer or portable hard drive in your secure location.

Need Access To This Archived Data — 3

Since you've already saved all of these important keepsakes and documents to your portable hard drives, online file folders and placed backup copies in your safe deposit boxes, they should be very easy for you to access even if you are in your evacuation location, right?

That's what we thought!

If you've chosen to save these keepsakes on a secure password protected server or password protected Cloud-based server, like Dropbox, iCloud or Sky Drive and place the link to those folders in a special contact on your smartphone. That way if you want to pull up some photos, or music, just make sure that everything is safe, you can just click the link on your smartphone and you'll have all the access you need.

When It Comes To Money, Never Assume...

A true story.

A minister and her husband had been great friends with another couple for many years. When the friend's husband died, the minister was surprised to find the wife waiting for her a few weeks later, in her office. The woman had been crying and was clearly distraught. The couple was older and the husband, though successful in business, had always lived frugally. The wife had come for prayer, because although she had been through all his papers, all of his accounts, his desk, everything, she realized that they basically had almost no money. This didn't make sense to her and it definitely didn't make any sense to the minister. This man might have been a little eccentric, but he loved his wife dearly and she couldn't ever imagine him leaving her destitute. Neither could his wife, but from all appearances…

The minister prayed with her friend. Before she left, the minister asked if there were any safe deposit boxes anywhere. Well, the woman said she had found one key, but wasn't certain what it opened. She told the woman to go to the bank and at least check it out.

The next day, the woman bounded into the minister's office with a huge grin on her face. It had taken a while at the bank to figure out which safe deposit box belonged to her husband, but once they did, the woman opened the box and found $200,000 in it – in cash! The minister hugged her. They were so happy that this dear friend wouldn't have to suffer financially in her old age. But the more the minister thought about it, she kept having this feeling that there was more money someplace. The husband was just too successful, only to have $200,000. She hated to get her friend's hopes up, but she had to tell her. The friend walked back out the door with renewed energy. Two days later, the minister got a call. After checking out every bank in the city, she found another box with an additional $150,000 – in cash.

The moral of the story?

Just because you know where all of your accounts, safe deposit boxes and investments are, doesn't mean your spouse or your family will. If this woman hadn't had a smart minister, with some "inside knowledge" to nudge her on until she found that money, she might have died destitute. Don't make your family play detective – especially when you're unavailable to fill in the details. THAT is what your Financial and Insurance Forms are for! Use them!

Secrets From The Experts

The Inside Story On... Neat Desk

With all the disasters that have taken place the last few years, Neat Desk is quickly becoming known for the ability to save its customers from dire situations. Kevin Garton, Chief Marketing Officer of Neatco, recently filled us in on all the details.

Neat Desk was originally created as a way to simplify paperwork, especially the drudgery of expense reports. It all started because the development team at Neatco was tired of having to gather their expense receipts, enter them into Excel, calculate everything manually and then copy, fax and mail them into headquarters, just to get an expense check. And they knew that they weren't the only workers who felt that way. So the first Neat Desk was created to scan receipts and expense documents with a portable scanner and into a laptop. Their invention immediately reduced cost and data entry. No more mailing, no more errors. Just one step and they were done.

Curious to see if Neat Desk would strike a chord with other executives, Neatco began installing Neat Desk scanners at airport retail kiosks. Executives from coast to coast loved it and encouraged Neatco to add more features. If it can do receipts, then what about business cards or tax information?

What sets Neat Desk apart from regular scanners is that it actually reads every document that is scanned into it and translates it into text with Optical Character Recognition. Once you scan your documents and save them to the Neat Desk database on your computer, you can easily find them by searching for any key word in the document. Just try to do that with a traditional file cabinet!

Before long, the newest generation of Neat Desk arrived, with the desk-sized Neat Desk and the portable Neat Scanner. The instant we tried Neat Desk, we were impressed. When we put a business card into Neat Desk it read the card and put all of the information on it – the name, title, phone numbers, and email address – right into the Neat Desk database on our computer. You can feed about twenty cards at a time, and the information pops up not only with a scan of the card, but with all of the contact information in the database ready to use any way you want. If you have two or three hundred business cards, they can be in your contact list in about fifteen minutes, without having to hit a single key!

And it does the same thing for receipts. When we scanned a drugstore receipt, it showed up in the database seconds later with the name of the store, items purchased, method of payment and whether or not the item was eligible for a flexible spending account. Imagine what this will do for your receipts at tax time. The regular sized Neat Desk can also scan both sides of a two-sided document simultaneously and in full color.

Customers love it, not only for the things we've mentioned but for scanning children's artwork, vital documents, business records, photos and even recipes.

Now every time she gets ready to cook dinner, she takes her computer to the kitchen with her! No magazine clippings or messy recipe cards, just a completely organized recipe database ready to go, anytime she needs it. Other customers have used Neat Desk to save their treasured photos and keepsakes, to preserve them for their own children.

The nicest thing of all is to be able to get rid of all those paper receipts cluttering up your file cabinets and drawers. And even if you do need to keep them for reference, you'll feel better knowing that you have a copy of them in the archive in case something happens to the originals.

Which brings us to disaster preparedness. Neatco has received letters from many customers, who tell them that their Neat Desk not only saved their family, but their business, after all of their business files were destroyed in disasters. One family in particular, whose home and home business were both destroyed in Hurricane Katrina, said that without Neat Desk, they wouldn't have a business. Just before the storm came, they had purchased a Neat Desk and had just finished scanning all of their receipts, business cards and documents. They took the Neat Desk and their PC with them when they evacuated, and because they had the documents they needed, they were able to get their business up and running again, in record time.

As cutting-edged as Neat Desk scanners are, it's only the beginning. Coming soon, Neat will be adding two new mobile services to the Neat Desk family. Neat Cloud is a cloud-based digital filing system that can be used in conjunction with Neat's desktop software to give customers the ability to automatically back up and access their important information from any web browser. Neat Mobile is a mobile app that allows customers to use their smartphone or tablet to 'scan' (via camera) and store information in their Neat Cloud digital filing system.

And to think it all started with an expense report.

For more information or to purchase your own Neat Desk, go to www.neatdesk.com.

The Inside Story On... Dropbox

Dropbox is a free online file cabinet that puts you in direct touch with all of your vital documents, vital information, photos, music and even your contacts whenever you need them, wherever you are. It was founded in 2007 by Drew Houston and Arash Ferdowsi, two MIT students tired of emailing files to themselves, so they could work from more than one computer. They set out to create an online filing cabinet, that would let them easily work on or share their documents via the internet, on any computer. And that's how Dropbox was born.

How does it work? When you go to Dropbox.com and set up a free account, you receive your own password protected online file cabinet, which you can use any way you want. Let's say you want to use your Dropbox as an additional backup location for your pictures, music, emergency plans and Grab It And Go Forms. When you download the Dropbox app onto your smartphone, tablet, PC or Mac, you will be able to access all of the files in your Dropbox. So if you're sitting in the ER with your child, you can easily grab his medical history to give to the doctor, while you're waiting. Or you could access all of your treasured photos and vital documents on your aunt's computer in your evacuation location, even though your main computer is two states away. And if you need to edit a document, you can make the updates and upload it back to Dropbox so that the updated version will be waiting for you back on your home computer.

It's also great for sharing information. If you have a family member who needs a document right away, they can just grab it from your Dropbox – as long as they have your password. Using Dropbox gives you the ability to have the latest copy of your documents without having to go searching for it on your computer or your phone.

If that weren't enough, Dropbox and their 14 million users are always coming up with new ways to use their technology to share information, especially during disasters like the Japan earthquake. But we'll let them tell their story...

"Like the rest of the world, we've been captivated by the events surrounding the earthquake and tsunami in northeastern Japan. While it's inspirational to see how technology has helped many in Japan quickly find and communicate with loved ones, the many uses of Dropbox that have been crafted to aid Japan's recovery, continue to amaze us.

- Following the earthquake, many of Japan's railways were delayed or inoperable. One clever person took it upon himself to aggregate Twitter streams mentioning any of Japan's major rail lines, then host the page out of his Dropbox. This resulted in a quick and easy way for thousands of Japanese locals to have up-to-the-minute tweets on the status of the nation's transportation. Since its launch, this page has been viewed several hundred thousand times.
- Dropbox was employed by the disaster committee of the Tohoku earthquake to allow more than 50 professionals to share information and photos for analysis of the hardest hit areas of the disaster.

- With many pieces of information becoming available every second from multiple sources, it was difficult to get the full breadth of news related to the earthquake and tsunami. Another brilliant group (of people) developed a page that aggregated Japan's primary news channels and Twitter streams to provide a steady stream of information related to the incident, to reach people without television.

What we're finding is that it's increasingly easy for a single person to work with Dropbox to affect and help many lives, and we're very honored to have played a role."

Dropbox has proven to be much more than a place to save files. It's become a virtual lifeline to millions, struggling to recover from unimaginable circumstances.

For more information about Dropbox, go to www.dropbox.com.

The Inside Story On… HP All In One Printer/Scanners

HP doesn't just create printers, they create solutions.

That fact couldn't be more evident that looking at their latest all-in-one printer/scanners, the Photosmart e-Station, the Office Jet Pro and the Envy.

When I spoke with HP's Andy Lisoskie I found out that there was a reason that the newest line of scanners suddenly appeared on the market. And that reason is Grandma. HP created these solutions with one thing in mind – helping families scan, print and share their lives through photos, whether or not every member of the family owns a computer or is even technically proficient.

So how did Grandma get into the picture? HP employees began to realize that many of their older relatives were feeling left out of all of the recent technological advances. While millions of people are out posting their photos on Facebook, their videos on YouTube or emailing pictures of the new baby the minute it arrives, their aunts, uncles and grandmas are missing out on sharing the joy. They're at home waiting for a printed photo that they can stick on the refrigerator. And let's face it, after emailing and posting photos, it's very easy to forget to do the traditional announcements and photo-sending, that provides the rest of our family with a link to our everyday lives.

And that was the idea behind HP's newest feature, ePrint. ePrint technology gives each of the new printers its own email address, so that someone taking a photo of their daughter stealing home plate can email that print directly from their cell phone or wireless camera to Grandma's printer. Even though Grandma may not have a computer – or the technical know-how to open an email and print an attachment, her ePrint enabled printer, receives that photo and prints it out for her – no expertise needed. The photo goes up on the fridge, and she gets to share in the moment, just seconds after it happens. Talk about keeping families together!

With the latest printers, you can also send yourself documents from work or on the go, photos while you're still on vacation, or anything you might need. Just hit ePrint and the pictures or documents will be waiting in your printer when you arrive home.

The other reason we've chosen to feature HP, is the amazing quality of their scanners. All of these printers, scan everything from aging photos to vital documents magnificently. Although all scanners scan to at least 600dpi (which is the recommended setting to ensure a quality scan for things like photos), HP scanners have a clarity and a vibrancy both in image and in color that is unmatched. If you're trying to scan your old family photos so you can archive them or print backup copies, using one of the three printers pretty much guarantees that you will end up with a scanned image that has the quality you need to make an identical reprint, or to repair or color-correct old, damaged photos. A low-quality scanner will result in a low quality photo.

Scanning all your photos and vital documents, gives you another way to archive them, either by saving them directly to your computer or onto a flash drive right from the printer, so you can put them in another location for safety. Doing that one thing would have saved both Trace Adkins and Richard Branson a great deal of sadness earlier this year. Both of them experienced devastating fires in their homes that consumed their collections of treasured photos. No matter who you are or what kinds of resources you have, it's so important to take a look around your home and find ways to preserve the things that mean the most to you, in case the unthinkable happens.

That is what HP is so good at – giving us ways to do the things we need to do – quickly and easily.

Our favorite all-in-one printer, has to be the HP Envy, just because of its size, ease of use and portability. The Photosmart e-station All-In-One is a little bit bigger and comes with a 7 inch detachable screen, that looks and acts like a tablet. You can pop it off the printer and use it as a wireless eReader, anywhere in the house. With both of the scanners, you can save any scan to a computer, to a memory card, send it to a friend or loved one, or save it up in the cloud to Google docs.

For the largest jobs, Andy recommends the Office Jet pro 8500A. It's not only great for scanning pictures but for documents, because it has an automatic feeder of up to 25 pages at a time, can handle legal sized pages and has a duplex feeder, which enables you to scan both sides of a document at the same time.

The printers are almost as impressive as the work HP has done on behalf of disaster victims. A few years ago, the team at HP was proud to be a part of an episode of "Extreme Makeover: Home Edition," on the ground in New Orleans after Hurricane Katrina. HP opened a mobile command center and offered to scan and repair photos that had been damaged or ruined in Hurricane Katrina. It took days to scan the thousands of photos. The grateful people didn't really know what to expect, as the team handed back the cracked, water-logged prints. But untold man-hours and 500 HP employees later, every photo was repaired and sent back to its family. The work was so amazing that they put together a gallery of the restored photos juxtaposed with the originals. And that was only the beginning. The team sprang into action after the San Diego wildfires and this past spring, Snapfish, a division of HP, gave Snapfish members in Joplin free 4X6 photo prints of any photos that were destroyed in the tornado and needed to be replaced. Whether it's providing solutions to safeguard memories before a disaster, or restoring people's memories after a disaster, there's no doubt about it. HP always hits a home run.

For more information or to purchase HP printers, go to www.hp.com.

The Inside Story On The Pandigital Wand Scanner & Kodak Photo Scanner

Do you remember how excited you were when scanners first came out? I know we sure were. After years of trying to copy documents and photos, and ending up with grainy images that paled in comparison to the original, finally a photo could be put onto a scanning bed and a perfect replica would magically appear right on your computer. For those of us who wanted to preserve our old photos or needed to make an identical image of something, it was a miracle.

But years later, not only did we get used to scanners, we started realizing what they couldn't do. They could scan a flat picture, but they couldn't scan a slide or a negative. They could scan a bunch of photos at home, as long as you took them out of the frame, or photo album, but you couldn't pick up your scanner and tote it over to Grandma's house – along with your computer, the cables and extension cords needed to copy her photos, unless you had an SUV and help. And scanning a book? Forget about it!

Well those days have changed, thanks to Pandigital and their product partner Kodak. If you haven't seen the Pandigital Hand Scanner yet, you're in for a surprise. Instead of bringing the photos to the scanner, Pandigital lets you take the scanner to the photos, where ever they are and whatever container they are currently in – albums, boxes or yes, even in the frame. You've probably seen a couple of wand scanners out there, but the Pandigital tops them all. We recently spoke with Jason Topel to find out exactly what makes Pandigital the leading wand scanner in the industry.

Pandigital's overall goal is to make scanning so effortless, that people actually start archiving their photos and keepsakes from vital documents to their kid's artwork. But the more the designers at Pandigital thought about their goal, the more they realized that a run of the mill sheet-fed scanner wasn't going to cut it. It was too impractical. So they set out to build a better scanner, one without all of the traditional limitations. A scanner that works simply by rolling it over the document. Their first model was an immediate hit. People loved the idea that they would no longer have to peel their photos out of the album to scan – and probably end up tearing or ruining the photo. Now they could just scan the whole page, without even taking it out of the album!

A wand scanner is about nine inches long, and uses an SD card to hold anywhere from 2GB of memory to 16 or 48GB depending on the model and the SD card. When you want to scan something, you just have to put it on a flat surface and roll the wand over it to capture the image.

As successful as they were, Pandigital still wasn't satisfied. Problem was, the first models ran on AAA batteries and the rollers didn't always roll smoothly, resulting in bumps or skips while scanning, which doesn't always result in a perfect scan. So the company created a rechargeable version with a lithium battery and AC adapter. Then they improved them even more with the advent of Scan Right rollers, which adds not one but two smoother rollers for very precise scanning action.

The Pandigital 08 line, which we had a chance to try, is so smooth, we could glide it over a photo with one finger to do a perfect scan, unlike other brands, that make you push or pull the scanner along very slowly to get marginal results.

The other thing Pandigital did is to make their scanners rugged and easy to clean, no matter what you're scanning. "We wanted parents to be able to scan their kid's artwork," added Jason, "even if the artwork is macaroni and glitter!" Even with glitter or pieces of dust, all you really have to do to clean the scan track, is to shake it a little bit or dust it out with a clean cloth. Try that with a sheet fed scanner, where even a grain of dust can get into a roller and leave permanent smudges on the screen.

Which brings us back to the issue of practicality. The best part about wand scanners is that you can take them wherever the photos are. For example, if you have an aunt or uncle who won't let their precious photos out of their sight or their home for even one night, all you have to do is take the Pandigital over to their house, scan the photos to the onboard SD card, and the photos are yours. You don't even need to have a computer with you. Once you get home you can download them to your computer or a portable hard drive just to back them up, or you can share them with other family members who can't wait to get their hands on them.

But that doesn't help us scan our old slides, does it? Or those long forgotten negatives we have sitting around in dusty photo sleeves. Don't worry, that's where Pandigital's partner Kodak comes in. Although the Kodak Personal Scanner 461, may look similar to the wand scanner, it's completely different. It has a feeder for photos and documents, which can be helpful for some older photos that are more fragile, or smaller photos that are hard to hold onto while scanning. But the amazing part is that it has a little attachment that clips onto the scanner and lets you feed your negatives and the film from your slides into the scanner – where it turns them into full color digital photos! We found some slides from the sixties, took them out of the cardboard slide frame, fed them into the scanner and seconds later, they had been transformed into digital photos. Simply breathtaking!

Even though Pandigital and Kodak have wonderful tools to help you scan and archive your photos, they wanted to remind you that the most important part of preservation – whether it's old photos or new ones – is to remember to preserve them! So we asked Jason for a few hints. "The most important thing of all is to take your photos off of your camera or phone as quickly as possible. Otherwise you're just asking for trouble." Jason not only downloads his photos every few weeks, but he also scans them and saves them to multiple locations – just in case. Then he emails them to himself at multiple email addresses and when they arrive, puts them in a zip file and saves them.

One thing about Jason, his kids will never have to hunt around for photos of their childhood! Which is exactly what Pandigital and Kodak are shooting for -- making scanning and archiving effortless. They've definitely achieved what they set out to do.

For more information go to www.pandigital.com.

The Inside Story On... iMemories

Mark Rukavina is on a mission to get people to take their videos and movies out of those dusty old boxes, and transfer them to digital format where they can be seen, enjoyed and shared with family and friends, before they fade away.

That's why Mark created iMemories.com. iMemories is a company that exists to do one thing – preserve memories. His passion for the subject is contagious. How else do you explain the fact that, mere days after talking to Mark, we actually ordered one of iMemories Safe Ship boxes, carefully wrapped and padded our old movies, GPS locator on board, and shipped them all the way to iMemories in (gulp!) Arizona. That box of old Super8 mm films was sitting in our house for thirty years before we were willing to let go of them long enough to have the film transferred to DVD.

There is only one thing that would have pried those films out of our hands. Someone who understands what we were feeling, who comprehends what our memories mean to us and cares enough to create a company that has never lost or destroyed one piece of film. Someone who cares enough to send along a GPS device, right in the box so that in the very unlikely event that your films go astray, he and his staff will know precisely where they are with satellite accuracy. That passion and care describes Mark to a T. And our experience with them, the way they cared for our old movies and the beautiful job they did transferring them to video/DVD, couldn't have been better.

Mark Rukavina actually calls iMemories a magical business, because customers are so over the top about it. The idea behind iMemories is simple. People are so overwhelmed by all of the movies, videos and photos they have, in so many different boxes and locations, that they end up just leaving them until they "have more time" to deal with them. So iMemories makes it as easy as possible for customers, by sending them a box, into which that they can simply stuff all of their videos, film and photos – no labeling necessary – and ship to iMemories from their local UPS Store or Best Buy.

As anyone who has ruined videos will tell you, movies – especially videotapes have a shelf life. For videos it's only about 8 to 10 years. They begin to degrade pretty quickly. First the color goes, then the sound and before you know it, that first recital or wedding video is a garbled mess.

Although 8mm and Super 8 films last longer – about 30 to 50 years – it's very difficult to digitize film to preserve it without special equipment and difficult to share it with others without a projector. Does anyone even have a projector anymore?

In his first two businesses, Mark became an expert at putting media on the internet. Realizing that everyone wants to preserve memories in an easy-to-obtain, easy-to-share way, he put his idea and experience together and came up with iMemories.

The way iMemories works is simple. iMemories will transfer your 8mm, Super 8, videotapes and even photos, onto DVD. You can pack up your own movies, or order the Safe Ship box, with or without the GPS locator (an extra charge). Once your movies arrive, they are catalogued and a customer service person is assigned to manage your order from start to finish. They email you to tell you the length of each video/movie and the amount the transfer will cost. Once you okay the transfer, it's completed and the videos/movies, now digitized, appear in your very own, personal, online theater. It's pretty amazing to see those old movies on your computer. From there you can decide to have the videos placed on a DVD, you can download them from their website, or as many people do, you can just leave them online, so that you can watch them and share them with family and friends, even if they're not members.

To Mark's surprise, more than anything, people use their iMemories account to watch and share their videos. After the initial film transfer, customers only pay for the DVD or for long term storage.

Mark and iMemories want to change the fact that so many people keep storing all their media on social media sites. That's why it was so important to him, that iMemories has both a photo and video sharing site to give customers the experience that they wanted. And he also makes sure that the security and safety of each piece of film entrusted into their care is impeccable. There are at least two redundant copies on servers in two locations.

"What I set out to do is to say to customers who are stressed out about what to do with their photos and videos 'It's going to be okay and here's how to do it'. That's why we do the GPS tracker. Treasured videos are not the type of thing that if you lose, you can just send a check for $500. That won't begin to compensate for the loss." Mark takes a moment, before finishing. "People want their stuff," he adds quietly. "If we're not going to cherish our memories, then what are we? That's what it's all about."

When we asked Mark to share what he's learned about the importance of being prepared for disasters, he immediately started telling us about the boxes he's received, that are charred after fires. He and his staff have to pick through to find films and photos and restore what they can.

"Don't wait thirty years to send your movies in and end up with garbled or blank video. So many things are attacking this priceless stuff. And it's not only movies and videotapes. The explosive growth of smartphones with 8 megapixel cameras and HD video is a real game changer." That's why iMemories is thrilled to announce, that customers can now share and upload videos and photos through their new iPhone, iPad and Android apps. "Bottom line," says Mark, "you can now view your memories anytime and anywhere - on virtually any device. It's very fun and exciting."

Let's all start honoring our memories and iMemories is the perfect way to do it.

For more information or to sign up for iMemories, go www.imemories.com.

The Inside Story On... Rubbermaid

The aftermath of tornadoes, floods and fires are absolutely devastating to homeowners. With record numbers of storms and some amazingly stubborn wildfires, Americans had to contend with situations no one should ever have to experience. Whether it was in Alabama, Joplin or Arizona, one company's product saved the day again and again – the Roughneck Storage Container by Rubbermaid.

There's a good reason that Rubbermaid has been a staple in households since 1902. It provides consumers with products that work.

But no one could have imagined just how well they work, until they were put to the ultimate test, surviving F3 and F4 tornadoes. Customers have been using Rubbermaid containers for years, because they know they resist water, are tougher than most containers on the market and when they take their possessions out of them, they're always in good shape. That's because Rubbermaid puts their Roughnecks through drop testing, impact testing and manufactures their lids to fit tightly with a bit of an overhang that naturally protects the contents of the container from dirt or moisture seepage. And with containers ranging from three to fifty gallons, they fit perfectly in everything from cars, to garages and storage areas.

In the spring of 2011, Rubbermaid began to hear some of the most amazing testimonials in their history. A family who was cleaning up debris after F3 tornadoes in Central Arkansas found storage bins in their yard, that belonged to another family. Two were Roughneck containers and two were containers made by another company. Evidently the tornado picked them up from another home nearly a mile away, and slammed them down in another family's yard! The woman who found them was amazed to find that the competitor's storage containers were absolutely shredded – nothing at all was left inside. But the Roughneck containers? The lids were still on and everything inside was in pristine condition and able to be returned to their owner!

Testimonial after testimonial said the same thing. Flooded basements where nothing survived, except Roughneck containers found bobbing in the water. Everything inside was safe and dry – including all of the couple's wedding memories. A house fire that destroyed 60% of the contents of a home. But the clothes found inside a Roughneck container was fine, even though the containers had to be thrown away from smoke damage. Even though Rubbermaid is quick to say that their containers are not waterproof or indestructible, the stories are a great testament to a container that does an excellent job of keeping things safer under normal and not so normal situations.

And that's why we were so excited to hear about Rubbermaid's newest product, the Grab it and Go Organizer. It's the perfect portable organizer for your evacuation kit. Although made to be an organizer for your car, the Triple Cargo Organizer, has multiple sections and pockets, made out of mesh, that can hold an incredible amount of items and tools, like the items on your Ready In 10 Evacuation List.

With handles, three sections and pockets galore, it's the perfect size and shape to put next to your Evacuation Bin to use during an unexpected evacuation.

Erin Gentry, who handles public relations for Rubbermaid, gave us some great tips on preparing for disasters. The most important is label, label, label everything especially if you're not using the clear containers. Roughneck's have kind of a bumpy plastic exterior and if you have trouble getting labels to stick, she recommends using Brother P-Touch labels, duct tape or masking tape.

Since Erin and her colleagues live in cold, snowy country, they also recommend keeping a Roughneck container in the back of your car filled with supplies for emergencies away from home. You wouldn't believe the number of customer stories they hear from people who have gotten stuck in the snow or in storms, just trying to back out of their own driveway. The items in their Roughneck saved their lives until they were found and rescued.

Of course Rubbermaid is also known for its work in the community. Every time a storm rages Rubbermaid is there, donating water containers and Roughneck Totes to give storm victims the means to safeguard the keepsakes and clothing they have left. It's nice to know that no matter what has happened for the last hundred years, Rubbermaid has been helping families pick up the pieces – and keep them safe.

For more information or to purchase Rubbermaid products, go to the www.rubbermaid.com.

Spotlight On... Aaron Berger

Chances were excellent that Aaron Berger would end up being organized. Coming from a family with many siblings – one of them a twin brother – knowing where all of his personal possessions were at any given moment, was a matter of pure survival! And with that large a family, Aaron also learned the importance of being ready for any emergency, at a very young age.

Both skills serve him well, in his current post as one of the resident Electronics Experts at HSN, the Home Shopping Network. Based in Florida, HSN brings the latest innovative, cutting-edge, electronics to millions of viewers twenty-four hours a day. With the world of computers, printers and tablets changing daily, understanding the newest gadget, let alone having to explain it, can be a daunting task. The fun part about watching Aaron in action is the ease with which he communicates the most intricate technology. After fifteen minutes with him, even the most technophobic viewer understands how to hook up a new printer to Wi-Fi, or why this camera will capture her son's slide into home plate, better than another one.

But the most unexpected lessons of his job, are those taught by viewers who have impacted his life with their own stories and experiences. Since Aaron's areas of expertise are cameras, computers and hand-held personal scanners, the viewers who call into his segments, are often purchasing the product he's selling, to fix the aftermath disasters have had on their lives.

For example, the people who call in to tell him stories about boxes of photos reduced to ashes in fires or waterlogged in floods. Or the people who are buying video cameras, because they lost their grandparents before they were able to get them on camera sharing some of their favorite family stories and want to make sure that the same thing doesn't happen with the next generation.

Every story has its impact not only on the other viewers and hosts, but on Aaron, who has made it his mission to help everyone he knows, back up or archive the things that are important to them, before it's too late. When people ask Aaron what he would do first, to get organized, he always starts by recommending his favorite wand scanner, the VuPoint. "I think the worst thing is the people who have lost their photos," says Aaron. "I can't tell you how many people have told me that they only wish they had bought their scanner sooner. They didn't prepare and they lost all of their photos or keepsakes in a fire or flood. Such heartbreaking stories that could have absolutely been prevented."

As far as documents go, Aaron suggests that people keep at least one copy of everything that's vital to them – photos, vital documents, business papers – in the Cloud. "Use it to back up data as well," says Aaron. "And don't just leave all your data at home thinking that you'll be able to grab it if you have to evacuate. That's just not logical. What if you're not at home when an evacuation happens or if your data or keepsakes are in a part of the house that you just can't get to, in a disaster? Having a backup copy of everything you need outside of the home, only makes sense." Besides our favorite online file box Dropbox, Apple has just launched the iCloud for Mac users.

HP has just come out with something on their computers called SimpleSave and there is also an app called Syncables 360, that syncs the data on your phone and tablets with your PC.

As far as archiving valuable documents, Aaron knows quite a bit about it. He lost his grandmother and grandfather earlier this year, both at the age of 92. The dearly loved matriarch and patriarch left behind not only the legacy of stories and history, but their collections of family photos. One collection was immediately commandeered and scanned by Aaron's cousin, who put the photos on a CD and send a copy to each member of the family. But his grandma's collection was left with Aaron's mom. She called him immediately and said, "What do I do with all these pictures?" He told his mom to get the hand held scanner and is happy to say that all of those memories – even the ones still in their frames – are now archived for posterity!

Another invaluable electronic breakthrough that Aaron loves is the Eye-Fi wireless SD card. No more trying to remember to download your photos! Eye-Fi does it for you. "Market data says that it takes people on average, nine months to download the photos on their cameras," says Aaron, "which leaves them vulnerable to corruption, or accidental erasure. Eye-Fi changes all that, by backing up your photos for you, without you having to lift a finger. It's a real game changer."

All of the advice Aaron gives his viewers is wonderful, but watching him on HSN, made us wonder how much of these innovations he actually uses himself. Aaron laughed when I posed the question. "All of them! I'm not a paper person, so I absolutely use all of these things myself, especially my portable scanner, Eye-Fi and the Cloud. If you walked into my apartment right now, you wouldn't even think a person lived there. Everything that comes into my house gets scanned and preserved."

Thanks Aaron, not only for inspiring your viewers to give technology a try, but for giving so many of them back something that they desperately need. Answers.

The Inside Story On... Tide Loads of Hope

A lot of companies say that they help disaster victims. Tide Loads of Hope actually does it.

For the last five or six years, a new truck has appeared at the site of major disasters along with the ubiquitous disaster response vans, like the Red Cross or UNICEF. It's a brightly colored, oversized truck that always brings a smile to the faces of disaster victims. Once it parks, the side of the truck opens to reveal a row of bright, shiny high-capacity washers and dryers. T-shirt clad Procter and Gamble employees are ready to wash, dry, fold and gift wrap laundry before returning it to their owners, people who simply want to feel clean again.

Tide Loads of Hope helps disaster victims by bringing normalcy to people in the midst of chaos.

Who would have thought that a company could have changed so many lives with such a simple concept?

After Hurricane Katrina the team at Procter and Gamble, in charge of non-profit efforts met to find a way that they could help people impacted by this and other storms. One thing that bothered them, was the fact that the basic needs of the hurricane victims were being met, but only their _most_ basic needs. They realized that once needs like water and first aid are taken care of, people need other things that are just as vital. Like having clean clothes.

They came up with the idea of using the Tide brand to clean victim's laundry, a simple concept that no one could have predicted would end up being such an enormous success. Just a few hours out of their day would give disaster victims another step towards normalcy. First though, they had to figure out how to do it. The team found a beer truck that was out of service and retrofitted thirty-two high-efficiency washers into it. Next they set up a partnership with Feeding America, that put them right in the middle of the disaster zone. By the end of their first on-site disaster, the team was hooked. Since then Tide Loads of Hope has been on the scene of dozens of disasters, starting with the San Diego fires.

Logistically, getting trucks and washers to the site of any disaster could easily be a nightmare. Since that first disaster, the P&G team has created a three-tiered system to decide which disasters need their direct attention with Loads of Hope trucks and which can best be served by just partnering with laundries in the area to wash and fold the clothes, or even simply sending product to help out. When the trucks are on site, 60-65% of the people handling the laundry are Procter and Gamble employees who volunteer to help out – the rest local volunteers from the area, looking forward to a new way to serve their neighbors and their community.

Loads of Hope has been so successful that two other types of trucks are now appearing at the site of international disasters – like the Haiti and Japan earthquakes – Duracell batteries and Pampers.

The Duracell truck not only provides batteries after disasters, but it gives people the ability to make phone calls and use charging stations to charge up their electronic devices like cellphones, portable radios and televisions or computers.

One thing that Loads of Hope has received from the beginning is grass roots support from Procter and Gamble customers. People love the idea that the money they pay for toothpaste or soap, goes to a company that is focused on changing the lives and circumstances of disaster victims. In just a few years, Loads of Hope's Twitter and Facebook pages have gained more than 2 million fans. P&G is using this attention to drive the need for disaster preparation for all of its customers, through partnerships with Ellen DeGeneres and Maria Menunos and with washing machine manufacturers like LG, Whirlpool and GE .

For Kash Shaikh, the experience of working with Loads of Hope has not only transformed his career, but his life. Kash oversees the international arm of Tide Loads of Hope, which often puts him right in the middle of the action. He loves the fact that the global part of their enterprise has been able to renew a sense of hope to countries devastated by unthinkable disasters. It also keeps Kash and his team on their toes. For example, when a his team found out that a hospital in Haiti had no way of cleaning the linen that they were using for wards full of injured earthquake victims, they had to step in and began providing laundry service for the entire hospital.

"We named our effort "Loads of Hope" because consumers kept telling us how much hope it gave them to see the smiling faces of people being presented with a clean stack of laundry." It fits right in with the motto of P&G's social project efforts -- Live, Love and Thrive. P&G has even been giving customers a way to be involved with the effort. Specially marked bottles of Tide feature the faces of the people that Loads of Hope has helped and a portion of the proceeds of those bottles goes to help those people and their communities. One of the most popular customer promotions has been vintage Tide Loads of Hope t-shirts, which can be purchased from their website.

The whole undertaking of Loads of Hope has really helped Kash shape his own purpose. "It helped me appreciate my life and loved ones more. I've seen people who just lost their loved ones, their homes and everything they have, and yet they got back on their feet. It's made me appreciate the resiliency of the human spirit."

Would you like to help Loads of Hope? To get involved and get connected, go to Facebook.com/tide.

Spotlight on… Kelli Ellis

Celebrity Interior Designer and Design Psychology Expert, Kelli Ellis never takes disaster preparedness lightly. Having spent her life in Southern California, she knows how important it is to make homes ready for anything, not only for her design clients, but for her own home which she shares with her husband and daughters.

We first saw Kelli on TLC's Clean Sweep, where she worked closely with Peter Walsh putting her skills as a design psychologist to work, to help people emerge from the clutter that kept them from getting on with their lives. Miles away from the all of the current shows about hoarders, Kelli and Peter managed to get people back on track in just a few days, not only getting rid of the clutter, but redesigning the areas of their homes that had been affected by piles of bags, boxes and sometimes even trash.

Many of the people on the show had something very important in common. They never had a clutter problem until they had a disaster in their lives. Whether it was a disaster like a house fire or the loss of someone close to them, holding on to whatever was left, became more important than going on with their lives. Kelli had some wonderful perspectives to share on that subject as well as ways to make sure your home and keepsakes are well protected in case disaster strikes.

Kelli, why do people sometimes begin to hoard possessions after experiencing a disaster?
"After experiencing a dire sense of loss, people sometimes start holding on to things and don't let them go, to stay in control. Like the depression, for example. I had a great grandma who suddenly began collecting things most people would think were crazy, like soap and paper, trying to dispel her sense of loss."

You did an amazing job of getting people to let go of their clutter and go back to living, back when you were on "Clean Sweep". How do you get them through it?
"I realized that to people who suddenly begin to have clutter, for example, after the loss of a loved one, things become the memory of the loved one. What I try to do instead, is help people choose what to keep of that memory and honor it, instead of the item. The item itself doesn't create anything, it's just an item. I recently had a client who lost her mother and found herself unwilling to give anything of her mother's away, including old clothes and furniture she clearly had no room to keep. I'll (pick up an item and) ask my client, "what does this mean to you?" Instead of letting my client keep a faded, worn out dress that her mother gave her for her graduation, I helped my client find a photo of her and her mother and the dress, and keep that instead.

Did that help?
It sure did! I've found that people who do this feel that if they give anything away, they feel like they're dishonoring the person's memory, so as a design psychologist, I help them feel better, by helping them create another memory instead. My client wouldn't give away her mother's furniture, but she had no room to keep it. So I found a family who had a fire and lost everything and arranged to give the furniture to them.

It was like giving her mother's furniture a new life with a new family. My final step was to have my client go and see the furniture in the new home and when she realized how much the family loved and appreciated it, it helped her gain the closure she needed."

Those breakthroughs are one of the many reasons that so many life and disaster coaches are taking Kelli's Design Psychology program. We also asked Kelli for some of her favorite tips for preserving keepsakes during disasters.

To keep breakables intact in earthquakes, the secret is to keep the bookcase or cabinet that holds them, from toppling over. The easiest way to do this is with QuakeHold Furniture Safety Straps that secure heavy furniture to the wall, preventing them from tipping over and injuring people or breaking the glassware inside. QuakeHold Straps even come in colors that match wood furniture. For breakables, Kelli puts QuakeHold museum wax on the bottom of the object to secure it to the floor of the bookcase or cabinet and also on the back of it to secure it to the back wall. This way, in an earthquake the object will stay secure no matter whether the earthquake is a strike/slip or a thrust fault.

For keeping photos safe in albums, without color change or damage, Kelli only uses albums that are both acid free and photo safe. "You'll know if they are, because if they are both acid free and photo safe, they'll have to say they are," says Kelli. "And if you don't have the right kind of album, simply keep your photos in the envelope that the store gave you when you had them processed. All stores use envelopes now that are absolutely photo safe." For photo boxes, Kelli uses the Aaron Brothers brand.

When we asked Kelli about some of her scariest disaster moments, the first one she thought of was a friend's recent experience, with a house fire. They live in a large canyon home with second story open to the rafters. The parent's room is on one side of the second floor and the children's on the other. When a fire started in the top of their home and the rafters gave way, essentially cutting the parents off from the children. The only thing that saved the kids were the emergency ladders on the children's bedroom windows. "I want to remind all your readers to install emergency ladders for all second story bedroom windows and to take the time to train your kids and family how to use them, so that it becomes second nature," says Kelli.

But her scariest moment happened during a recent ten hour blackout in Orange County. "I was driving through Laguna Beach, on PCH when the lights went out and all the stores were closed because there was no power. I suddenly realized that no one had any way of getting money for essentials – none of the registers worked, no ATMs nothing. It was scary wondering what would happen if I were to run out of gas before I got home. I had an earthquake kit in my trunk, but no food or water. It really made me realize how important it is to keep an emergency stash of cash at home and something to eat in my car, just in case."

Thanks Kelli for the great advice and we wish you continued success with all of the amazing work you do.

The Inside Story On... Adobe Photoshop Elements

Have you ever opened an old photo album from the sixties, only to find that the once vivid, brilliant colors you remembered had turned into washed out pastels? Or the beautiful Kodacolor shots of your childhood or your kids taken in the seventies and eighties are now a mottled mess of brown and orange?

We've been there! And no matter how carefully you stored those treasured prints, the old plastic in the albums somehow conspired with the acidic paper (state of the art at the time) to make your favorite pictures nearly unrecognizable.

So what do you do, just live with fading memories? Not anymore! We have family photos from the twenties to the eighties that needed help. Some were brilliant black and white with minor scratches and tears. Some were the aforementioned photos from the seventies that had turned an ugly shade of squash. We tried everything and finally had to turn to the experts at Adobe to get a few hints on restoring color gone wrong.

Correcting photos quickly and easily is one of the main reasons that Adobe created Photoshop elements 10, its latest easier to use cousin of the high velocity Adobe Photoshop.

Basically Photoshop Elements 10 uses your computer to analyze your photos color, contrast, hues, highlights, brightness right nest and helps you correct them to a state as near-normal as possible. It works in two ways, either automatically with quick fix, where you literally push a button and the software analyzes the photo and makes the changes it deems necessary or it can work with you to make adjustments in any of the areas we mentioned plus hundreds more. In other words, it gives you as much or as little guidance as you need to correct your photos.

The biggest problem is the photos themselves. Any photo software can only work with the color that's left in the picture, to enhance it. So if the photo was left out on a wall or in light for a long time or if the colors broke down – that happens a lot with Kodachrome from the 50s that turn purple and blue – there may not be enough color left of the picture to correct it.

According to Bob Gager, an Adobe project manager who helped build the PSE 10 software, this version is better than ever at automatic, quick color correction. Your first step should always be Auto Quick Fix, to see how the software does at fixing your picture automatically. Compare it to the original and if it's close to the original colors, or just needs a little adjustment, great! If it's really off, you'll have to be a little more hands-on to fix it, so just undo the quick fix and start over.

Let's take faded, pale photos from the 60s for example. We found that they're usually missing red and blue, as well as lacking a true, dark black. Since the software fixes photos by balancing the darkest black point, lightest white point and great, that can be a problem!

So what works? We found that starting with Quick Fix brings back a good deal of color, then we use "adjust the skin tone", which works by clicking on anyone's skin with a little eyedropper tool. Then adjust the highlights to darken the shadows a bit, bringing up missing details. We found a cousin in one photo whose face was hidden in the shadow! Finally we bump up the red and blue saturation in the photo, until it looks as natural as possible. For play-by-play instructions on fixing 60s photos, go to our website.

Photoshop Elements also makes editing black-and-white photos, tears and all, much easier. With the healing brush and spot brush you can literally wipe scratches, tears and spots away with a swipe of your mouse.

Another plus with Elements is that you can back up your photos online, something Bob Gager told us he wished he had had a few years ago, when his PC crashed, taking all of his child's digital photos from ages two to six along with it. That's what Photoshop Elements 10 is all about, creating ways for everyone technically-inclined or not, to be able to fix and preserve their photos quickly and easily.

For more information or to purchase Adobe Photoshop Elements www.adobe.com.

The Inside Story On... The Circa Address Book, by Levenger

Steve and Lori Leveen set out nearly twenty-five years ago to create a different type of store. A store where extraordinary leather bound notebooks and fine ink pens are the rule, not the exception. So it makes perfect sense that their store, Levenger, would be the perfect place to go for a different kind of address book. An address book that actually grows and changes as quickly as your friend's contact information.

Have you ever finished filling in your beautiful new address book, only to learn a week later that one of your so-called friends just moved and changed all her contact information? The only way you can change that address is by putting in a new entry or scratching out the old one. No matter what, the page and your once pristine book, are ruined.

We sure have and so has Steve Leveen. That frustration gave Steve the idea to take the old medium we all know and love – paper – and update it for the twenty-first century, by giving us the ability to change an entry in our address book as often as our friend's numbers change, without messing up the rest of the book. It's called the Circa Address Book.

Circle notebooks have been around since World War II. If you haven't seen one, circle notebooks replace wire or ring binding with round, reusable discs, to create a notebook that isn't restricted by its binding. With a circle notebook, you get a cover and a back held together by the round discs. A small disc holds a small amount of paper and a larger disc a greater amount of paper. Since there is no binding, if you need to take out a page, you just remove it and replace it with another one.

Levenger's version of the notebook is called Circa, which is the basis for an entire system of organizers, including Behance. After talking to their customers, Steve realized they were as frustrated with traditional address books as he was, and that customers wanted a flexible solution. So Steve and Lori created address book pages for their Circa notebooks. With Circa, not only can you replace an address book "page", but they went one step further by making every entry on the page perforated, allowing people to replace the whole page or just a single entry! Although notebook sales worldwide are on the decline, Levenger's sales are growing, mainly because of the design and flexibility of their notebooks.

Levenger's mission is to keep old technology alive by improving it with modern advances. Just as bicycles keep on evolving by adding new features and the latest technology, everything Levenger sells, stays fresh by incorporating new options and featuring the highest quality papers and inks their merchandising people can find.

One thing Steve and Lori stress is sustainability – and not just where address books are concerned. They have made a commitment to use reforested paper. Reforested paper takes environmental responsibility to a whole new level, not just by not using paper to save a tree, but to ensure that when trees are used, they are replaced. Trees and paper are harvested and planted like food and then they're re-cropped to begin a new twenty-year cycle of growth and harvest.

But will the notebooks last as long as the harvest? According to their customers, yes! "When you print things on the best paper possible," says Steve, "it will last an incredibly long time. In fact great quality paper, pressed tightly together remains strong even if it's scorched. It takes a lot of heat to go all the way through a notebook enough to destroy it." Evidently the same holds true with water. Many customers have written Levenger to tell them that they've dropped their notebooks in water, only to find that they survived. Between replaceable address entries, water and heat resistance, a new Levenger Circa address book, is the best thing since the Post-It Note!

For more information or to purchase Circa Notebooks, go to www.levenger.com

The Inside Story On... Verizon Wireless

The last few years our cell phones have become more than an accessory, they're often the link that connects us with the people, information and news that we need to get through the day.

When that connection is endangered – by a disaster, downed cell towers or loss – the link is gone along with everything that it brings us. The people at Verizon not only understand that, they plan for it, by doing everything they can to keep their subscribers connected with the rest of the world.

Since cell phones and smartphones perform so many functions in our lives, cellphone company's "backup plans" suddenly have taken on a whole new meaning. And until we spoke with Verizon's Thomas Pica, we had no idea how complicated a job, connection can be.

But how do you provide cell service, that keeps on working no matter what the emergency, to keep your customers up and running, no matter where they go?

The solution? Having so many redundant servers and if need be, additional cell towers to bring uninterrupted service to subscribers. In fact, Verizon has built such an outstanding record that emergency services like firefighters and have police turned to Verizon for help with their own communications.

Then there is internal backup – keeping the information that you put on your phone at your fingertips and enabling it to be restored if your phone is lost, stolen or if your data is accidently deleted.

That's where Verizon My Backup system comes into play. My Backup is a free service for all Verizon customers that literally backs up the contacts and data on your phone, to the cloud – in this case to the Verizon servers – providing one touch restoration. Verizon has also partnered with CBW, a company we mentioned earlier in the book that allows Verizon customers to make back up recordings of their important voice mail messages, archiving them, before they can be inadvertently deleted off the their phone.

But what really impressed us is the way that Verizon shines during emergencies. Moments after disasters strike, Verizon is on the ground with their Mobile Communications Centers working to reconnect their customers, help emergency personnel with communication needs, and providing assistance in any way that they can.

The mobile communication centers are equipped with fully functional phones, so residents without working cell phones can contact family, friends and loved ones, free of charge. The centers also feature Internet connectivity and a battery charging station to allow customers to charge their cell phones and smartphones.

Here in their own words, is Verizon's response to just one disaster – the floods in Minot North Dakota.

"In June 2011, the state of North Dakota faced record flooding, with the city of Minot under siege from the Mouse River…forcing the evacuation of more than 10,000 residents. The Verizon Wireless Network team added 55% more capacity to area cell sites and also deployed a Cell on Wheels (COW) temporary cell site for additional capacity. The company deployed more than 125 wireless devices to first responders and the Verizon Foundation donated $15,000 to the Mid-Dakota Chapter of the American Red Cross to assist those impacted by the flooding."

Verizon takes this work so seriously, that they actually send producers and directors out into the field after disasters occur, to capture their communications experts in action and to catch customer's experiences and success stories as they happen.

Talk about full service! Whether it's providing day to day connectivity with the top smartphones in the industry, or dealing with sudden disaster, when it comes to being there for its customers, Verizon always goes above and beyond.

For more information on Verizon, go to www.verizon.com.

The Inside Story On... Zomm

Zomm can not only save your phone, it can save your life.

Henry and Laurie Penix are a very talented couple who came up with an idea. As with any unique idea, it was born out of a need. We had the pleasure of speaking to Henry about Zomm, but first, here is Laurie's story.

"Every day while walking on the treadmill and watching Oprah, I prayed that God would send me an idea that will enable me to work smarter, not harder. During one of these workouts, one of my girlfriends called me and asked me if I had an extra mobile phone. Her husband had lost yet another one of their phones. What made this day special was that I had just finished reading an article on *Bluetooth*® technology. The article mentioned how this technology can be used to connect products within about a 30' distance. It was at this moment that I had what my husband, Henry, calls an 'exercise, Oprah-induced, epiphany.

Laurie and Henry have a history of successful ventures and have helped many other business leaders grow their companies. From her entrepreneurial experience, she knew this idea was special!

I told Henry my idea and we both became convinced that a "wireless leash™" product would be a solution to a very common, modern day problem. We immediately went online and searched *Bluetooth*® technology and the name Peter Hauser kept coming up over and over. We contacted Peter and invited him to our home in Tulsa to explore the idea further.

In the months that followed after the initial meetings with Peter, Zomm quickly grew from a concept to patents, drawings and specifications. Henry and I believed so strongly in Zomm and its potential that we made the decision to put all of our resources towards making Zomm a success.

With the team assembled, Zomm (the company) was born. What followed was arguably the fastest development project in history. Zomm grew from a concept to a functional, mass-producible, high-end consumer product in less than a year. In the process, Zomm won a prestigious CES Innovation Award in its category in 2010."

Henry is so passionate about Zomm that his enthusiasm is contagious. Whether on QVC or the newest Zomm commercial, the possibilities of this seemingly simple invention spring to life, every time Henry speaks.

Zomm, is the world's first Wireless Leash for mobile phones. The idea is simple. You sync Zomm to your phone electronically and clip the Bluetooth-enabled Zomm to your keychain. If you walk away, leaving your phone behind, Zomm will begin to flash, vibrate and if you don't pay attention to it, sound an alarm alerting you to go back and retrieve your cell phone.

Not only does it act as an alert for a forgotten phone, but it also lets you know if your phone is being stolen. So let's say you're really good about keeping tabs on your phone. That's when Zomm's other features come in handy. How many times have you been in the car when your phone rings, but you can't get to it. If it's at the bottom of your purse, briefcase or bag, there's just no way, short of pulling over, that you can safely retrieve your phone while driving. But your keychain? That's always right at your fingertips. All you have to do to answer a call (at least where that's still legal!) is click the Zomm and it turns into a crystal clear speakerphone.

One of the features that we love best is that the Zomm also comes with a panic button. When you get a Zomm, you can program an emergency contact number into it, that will dial a loved one or friend for assistance. In fact, you can also sound an emergency alarm to alert people around you, that you need help.

In fact, Zomm works so well, that Henry and Laurie's company began getting calls from 911 call centers. They sent help of course, but had no idea what the device was, that was calling them for assistance! So the people at Zomm began dispatching team members out to emergency call centers to show emergency responders what Zomm could do. They absolutely loved it. For years, people who had been in a car accident couldn't reach their cell phones to call for help. In an accident, cell phones usually go flying across the car, completely out of reach of the drivers or passengers. But since Zomm is at the end of their keychain, the panic button is usually within easy reach, making an enormous difference in getting assistance to accident victims, when minutes count.

Early in 2012, Henry and Laurie announced a new product that has already won three innovation awards at the Consumer Electronics show. It's a lifestyle connect device that gathers information constantly from people that need monitoring, or seniors with an alert system, that feeds the information into a hub that, when triggered can go to their emergency contacts, their caregivers, their doctors and brings all of that information into one place so help can come immediately.

As for us, we can't wait to see what they will come up with in the future!

For more information or to purchase Zomm, go to www.zomm.com.

The Inside Story On...Operation Blessing

Operation Blessing International (OBI) meets the needs of people after disasters, not by giving them whatever they happen to have available, but by listening to what the people need and then working to provide it. And that's when miracles begin to happen.

According to Bill Horan, OBI's president, disasters are as different as snowflakes, and how much they can do in a disaster depends on the severity of the disaster and the generosity of their donors. During one year, Operation Blessing International, a non-profit humanitarian organization with one of its six core competencies being disaster relief, responded to 41 disasters in 16 countries. In fact, the domestic disaster relief team was on the road non-stop for a record five months. We caught up with Bill, to find out how they've coped with major disasters from Japan, Haiti and a record number of tornadoes right here in the United States.

When a disaster strikes, Operation Blessing relies on cash and gift-in-kind donations to help bring emergency food, water and other critical relief to victims.

For the Japan earthquake and tsunami, Operation Blessing's donors responded enthusiastically, allowing them to be on the scene and providing strategic emergency relief in Japan within 48 hours of the disaster. Bill and his team noticed that other disaster relief organizations in Japan were following the media to Sendai, the epicenter of the tsunami. Knowing that people in Sendai were already getting a great deal of attention and help, the OBI team kept traveling up the devastated coast to Shiogama, tuna capital of Japan, where fishing is vital to their economy. With their boats and fishing equipment destroyed, many of these families were without the means needed to survive or rebuild.

After a major disaster, people are almost always in need of food, water and medical assistance. In the city in Shiogama, there was a need for rice, bottled water, and also kerosene to keep the temporary shelters warm that were housing displaced families. After these basic needs were met, Bill's team went to talk to the mayor. Operation Blessing is known for their practice of "ask don't tell."

"One non-profit will come on the scene and say, 'we'll build houses,' and another will say, 'we'll build roads,' " explains Bill. "That's wonderful, but what if the city or its people don't need those particular things. I've found that templates just don't work during disasters. It's amazing what you learn when you really listen." So the Operation Blessing team took out a notebook and asked the mayor of Shiogama what his town needed.

The first need the mayor mentioned had to do with the people who lived on the neighboring Urato Islands. The fishing families on the islands had food and water, but no electricity or internet communications. The mayor told OBI that they would be without power for a minimum of six months and therefore would be out of business within the fishing industry, which is their livelihood. So Bill immediately ordered 20 industrial-grade diesel-powered generators and had them sent to Japan via DHL.

Soon after that meeting the OBI team arranged for a boat and went offshore to meet with the Fishing Guild elders on one of the four Urato Islands. Bill asked the island community leaders to make a list of everything else they needed and to arrange the list in order of priority. One young guy on the leadership committee was very tech savvy. He came back to Bill with the following list: two computers, a wireless card, printers and office supplies. Why? The office for the Fishing Guild was the nerve center for the whole island. Because many people didn't have computers or generators in their own home, the fishing guild was the place where the whole town did their banking and shopping online.

The OBI team returned with all the equipment requested. The young fisherman was thrilled. He quickly designed a program that would allow town members to do everything they needed to do online. Then he also started an online Twitter campaign asking other Japanese people to give 10,000 yen (about $120 USD) to purchase vouchers for seafood where they would receive their product when the fishermen were back in business. Over 14,000 people responded and the campaign received about $2.2 million (USD).

During another visit with the community leaders, the Shiogama vice mayor took a pair of broken eyeglasses out of his pocket. He explained that many people rushing to escape the waves either lost or broke their glasses. In addition, many Japanese wear their contacts to work and leave their glasses at home. When the earthquake hit, their homes were washed away along with their glasses. So—Operation Blessing decided to do free eyeglass clinics. They found a Japanese optometrist and arranged for thousands of pairs of frames to be donated. The optometrist went out to the shelters with the OBI team, examined everyone's eyes and came back the next week with eyeglasses for everyone who attended. The simple act of someone giving away free eyeglasses just astounded them!

The most amazing thing about these stories is how far the seed that Operation Blessing plants, reaches. Whether money or goods or sweat equity, Bill and his team are determined to make a difference with what they have to give. For example, they committed $600,000 to the Urato Island project. Part of that went to the computer equipment that enabled the town to get the rest of the money they needed to rebuild and get the fishermen back on their feet. Then Bill's team was able to purchase 42 boats to help another fishing community. He first went to the Japanese boat makers, trying to keep the work and the money in Japan, but they were already overwhelmed with orders after the earthquake. So Bill took the money that was donated for boats and turned to a company in Maine that had been having a hard year due to the economy in the U.S. The company had just laid off all of their people, but this one order put the entire company back to work.

It's just seed after seed, meeting need after need, whether in the disaster region or here at home. "When you operate in the mode of sowing seed," says Bill, "it's amazing how everything just comes together and how it works." For more information on Operation Blessing, go to www.ob.org.

The Inside Story On... State Farm Insurance

Have you ever noticed that every commercial for homeowners insurance or car insurance is the same? A family suffers a sudden disaster or loss, and ends up sitting on what is left of their house, or a woman sits staring into a camera and tells a sad tale of her husband dying and leaving their family with nothing. Or how about the latest one – the guy who wreaks havoc in people's lives simply for the heck of it. No matter what the hook, they're all based on one thing. Scaring their audience into buying their insurance before it's too late.

It's all about fear.

All of that changed with the advent of Dwayne. Have you seen Dwayne? A twelve story robot/alien hybrid decides to take revenge on an unsuspecting neighborhood, one guy in particular. Dwayne. First the monster squashes his car, then it rips open his house and then it picks him up – recliner and all – and drops him right on the sidewalk, while his neighbors provide the play-by-play commentary. Finally they conclude, deadpan to the camera. "Wow, that thing really doesn't like Dwayne!"

Not a touch of fear, just silliness, but somehow, through the humor we get the message that State Farm is there for anything life throws at us – even 12 story monsters! It takes the whole "like a good neighbor" tagline into the 21st Century. And when we spoke to State Farm's Holly Anderson, we found out why. To State Farm, being a good neighbor isn't just a tagline, it's a way of life.

Take the tornadoes of 2011. State Farm responded to the unprecedented, spate of tornadoes with the biggest catastrophe team they've ever assembled. When a tornado, earthquake or other disastrous event strikes, the company dispatches their mobile work force to the area, not only to help homeowners file insurance claims, but to give them whatever assistance they can, to get the family and their home back on track. Disaster response starts back at the State Farm command center, where experts constantly monitor radar and storm trackers, so the team can respond, the moment they're needed. The mobile work force arrives in a vehicle that looks like a semi on the outside, but is fully outfitted inside with everything their team needs to serve their customers and rest in-between shifts. The truck is updated often to help the team meet the ever-changing needs of its customers. Recently added, was its own Wi-Fi system, so that the force will no longer have to rely on finding local access to high-speed internet.

In Holly's words, "We can't ask our customers to be prepared if we're not!"

Take the story of State Farm's agents in Joplin. When the devastating tornadoes struck Joplin, his own home was among the rubble. One he made sure that his loved ones and neighbors were all right, the agent made his way to his office. Miraculously it was untouched by the storm.

He walked in, cleaned up a bit and started pulling his customer files to get a jump on what he was certain, would be a long line of customer claims. There was a knock at the door and then another as customers came by, not to file claims, but to make sure that he was okay, or simply because they had no place else to go. That's when the agent decided to open his office – now his makeshift home – to his customers, letting them clean up, share food or get some sleep until they were able to get emergency assistance. When the State Farm mobile work force arrived, he was able to hook up his computer to get the claim's process started both for his customers and himself.

Of course that's just a small part of the State Farm story. Agents going above and beyond, to help clients restore their homes and lives. Employees giving their weekends to work for disaster relief. State Farm Back with its free online full service checking account, giving customers 24-7 access to their money, wherever they are in the U.S..

Keeping even a little money at State Farm Bank is smart, because it's there for you, when your local back may not be. A local bank can be impacted by the same emergency as your home and is just as vulnerable to electronic outages or floods or disaster damage. At State Farm Bank on the other hand, you can take money out of ATMs where ever you are and they'll rebate any fees incurred. Or you can bank online in an emergency, from a relative's computer, cell phone, tablet or even cash a check with their mobile app.

Since State Farm Insurance has been giving clients disaster advice for decades we asked Holly to share some of her favorite tips.
- Review your homeowner's disaster coverage with your agent, to make sure everything is covered before a disaster.
- Protect your property by keeping a stock of plywood and materials, to board up windows or secure things around your property.
- Move garbage cans into the garage before a storm, so they don't go flying around and breaking windows and don't forget to secure your boats and cars.
- Create your family's evacuation plan, and decide where you will go and if need be, where your evacuation shelters are located. If you don't know where they are, call your local police or fire department now for that information.

And consider larger disaster upgrades like installing impact resistant roofing storm shelters, and a whole house detection system for things like methane or carbon dioxide. Detection systems can also measure the water pressure in your home, to prevent burst pipes. You might even be able to get a discount on your insurance after making these kinds of upgrades.

"I always tell customers that there is a lot you can do to get prepared in one hour, one day or one weekend," says Holly. "Just jump in and get started."

We couldn't have said it better ourselves! Want to see the making of the State Farm "State of Chaos" commercial? Go to: http://www.youtube.com/watch?v=F1TRNKxVgUA
For more information about State Farm, go to www.statefarm.com

The Inside Story On... Eye-Fi

An Eye-Fi SD card may look just like a regular 4 or 8 gigabyte memory card, but that's where the comparison ends. When you use an Eye-Fi SD card into your digital camera or video camera, Eye-Fi not only saves the pictures, but once you return home, it sends those pictures or videos directly to your PC for back up, via your Wi-Fi network. No more having to remember to upload the pictures to your PC, or trying to find the USB cord so you can hook the camera up to your computer.

In a world where people regularly take as long as nine months to actually take the photos out of their cameras and do something with them, that's practically a miracle. As Eye-Fi founder Ziv Gillat explained, the idea for this little SD card came from a real life problem.

Back at the end of 2005, Ziv found himself in an interesting predicament. Married, with a new baby, Ziv, a photographer by trade, had moved to Mountain View California to work on a few internet startup companies. Mountain View, home of Facebook, Google and Apple, were going strong, but he was trying to find the right fit or the right product. But life goes on even when people are extraordinary busy, and Ziv's mother, living on the other end of the country, wanted to see pictures of her grandchild – regularly. Ziv and his wife had little time to take pictures but even less time to upload them to the PC and email them to their parents. As he says, cameras are fun to use, but getting the pictures out of them wasn't so easy.

Ziv's business partner was having the same problem. Every time he shot professional photos, he'd end up with high resolution photos that produced huge files and were a pain to have to save or send to other people. So they decided to find a way to cut out the middleman and create a memory card that transmits the pictures from your camera to your computer for backup or shares them with other people, without having to lift a finger. That's how Eye-Fi was born.

But as inventions often do, this one picked up a few other innovations along the way and Eye-Fi not only sends pictures to the computer across the room via your home Wi-Fi network, it also transmits photos from any Wi-Fi hotspot to your home computer or even to Facebook and Picassa for instant sharing. So if you're on vacation in Hawaii and just took a bunch of photos, you can stop in a Starbucks or your Wi-Fi enabled hotel room and literally beam your photos home. There are three huge benefits to this. First, you'll have the pictures saved to another location, so you can delete them from your camera, in case you're getting low on memory space. Second, in case something happens to your camera while you're traveling you'll still have your photos without having to rely solely on your camera to preserve those memories. If you're not around a Wi-Fi hot spot, the card can actually become its own Wi-Fi hotspot and will transfer files to your nearby smartphone.

But the third benefit is the most interesting. A couple who was vacationing in Florida, stopped to have dinner and didn't realize until they had already left the restaurant, that their camera bag – camera and all – was missing. They looked everywhere but couldn't find it. Luckily, they had an Eye-Fi card and had backed up their photos with a Wi-Fi connection, so at least they would have their photos. Two weeks later, the woman noticed that there were some photos she didn't recognize in her Eye-Fi folder. More of them started to appear and she realized that they weren't her pictures. They were pictures being taken by the person who stole their camera. On closer inspection she recognized one of the people in the picture. The waiter from the restaurant. The police were able to use the geo-locator information on the new pictures from Eye-Fi to track him down, arrest him and get the camera back. Now THAT is a full service memory card!

As a disaster prevention tool, Eye-Fi is wonderful, because it ensures that the photos you take will be saved in a location other than your camera, even if you don't remember to upload them right away. Eye-Fi goes a step farther to help you preserve your photos by offering storage in the Cloud for customers. "Don't just have your pictures on a PC because PCs usually eventually crash," says Ziv. "Friends of mine lost all of the photos of their children because their PC crashed and they didn't have them backed up anywhere else." That's one of the reasons they began offering no-limit Cloud storage for Eye-Fi customers. For five dollars a month or fifty dollars a year, being able to save your photos to the Cloud, directly from your camera is a great way to ensure that your memories are safe.

For Eye-Fi, the future is getting brighter and brighter. The company has strategic partnerships with ten camera companies and the two top Japanese wireless companies to pre-bundle their apps with new cell phones. Although Eye-Fi works in any camera, the cameras from the partner companies are pre-enabled for Eye-Fi cards making the Wi-Fi transfer faster and smoother.

But for Ziv it's all about the customer. "I love it when customers say how wonderful it is, not to have to stress out over their photos. Because when they use Eye-Fi, everything is taken care of."

For more information about Eye-Fi, go to www.eye-fi.com.

The Inside Story On… OnStar

Fade In: ON an SUV driving down a highway. The man behind the wheel, enjoying a beautiful drive on a cloudy day. Suddenly his wheels hit a skid. Before he knows what's happening, the day takes a tragic turn as the man tries with all his might to maintain control. He can't and the SUV races toward a cliff. He's airborne. All he can see is the river hurtling towards him at breakneck speed. Suddenly he hears a voice. It's the OnStar representative, saying that the sensors in his vehicle have alerted them that he needs help. He tells the representative what's going on. She tells him she's sending help. "When you hit the water," she yells, "try to get on top of your truck." "We're coming," are the last words the man hears before he hits the water. The operator's words resounding in his brain, the man scrambles out of the truck before it fills with water, and up to the roof. He stands there, best as he can, with nothing to do but ponder his fate. And then he hears it, the sound of a helicopter coming to his rescue, thanks to his truck's onboard GPS. The rescue workers pluck him from the roof and race him to safety. And we Fade Out.

The trailer for a new movie? No, just another day at OnStar.

OnStar, a division of General Motors, began as an idea in early 2001. Their goal was to design a way to always be there for their customers, whether that meant providing turn by turn navigation, road assistance, or help during emergencies and disasters. But their disaster capability is the thing that would be tested first. Just a few months after the service began, on a warm, sunny September morning, planes hit the World Trade Center. After 9/11, OnStar executives took six months to review and assess their operations, to decide exactly how to best serve their customers, no matter what the situation. By the time the blackout of 2003 hit New York and neighboring states, they had given America a lifeline that not only provided great service, but saved lives.

The secret of their success comes from the connectivity between headquarters, the OnStar Agents and their customers. For example, during a hurricane or tornado outbreak, headquarters is constantly updating the information appearing on their agent's computers, from live updates with local radar and weather reports. The agents are not only communicating with their subscribers to give them assistance – whether that is directing them around or out of a storm damaged area, sending tow trucks or emergency assistance – but they're also keenly listening to what their subscribers have to say. If a subscriber tells her agent that a road is washed out, or a funnel cloud just touched down at a specific location, the agent is able to relay that information back to headquarters, where it can be communicated to other agents, providing subscribers with a level of real time information, unavailable in other services. Always able to see the big picture, OnStar often knows more about what's going on, than the rescue personnel who are in the middle of it.

That also gives OnStar the ability to provide services that no one could have predicted, For example, no one knew just how bad Hurricane Katrina would be. One problem that became obvious as the storm raged on, was that people from New Orleans needed hotel rooms in neighboring cities and states.

As local hotels filled up, OnStar agents were searching for available hotel rooms in surrounding states, to which they could immediately direct subscribers. At one point they had to look as far away as Indiana!

When we asked Mary Ann Adams of OnStar exactly how they pull all of this off every day, she laughed. "A lot of practice," said Mary Ann. She went on to tell us that the connectivity for OnStar comes from the external antenna of the car, and through cell companies, which is one of the reasons that OnStar's connections work even when all of the electricity and cell towers are down. There was a story not long ago about a tornado survivor who had no way of calling her family to tell them she was okay and to check on them after the storm. Then she remembered that she had OnStar. She went to her car – the button connected and the operator was able to call her family and conference them in so she could talk to them through her car's speakers.

Disasters have proven to be the toughest situation for a service like OnStar. Not only do they have to help their subscribers evacuate an area if their homes are destroyed, but guide them to find shelter, food and water. That's not always as easy as it sounds. After a tornado hits, landmarks are gone, street signs are down and a normal evacuation center can be reduced to rubble. It can be so bad that people often get lost in their own neighborhoods. But with GPS, landmarks are unnecessary, so OnStar subscribers have a much easier time getting their bearings.

Which brings us to more traditional types of emergencies. Of course everyone knows that OnStar is great for calling tow trucks or checking on subscribers if they get an indication that their car has been in an accident. What you might not know, is that they're also there to help in other types of emergencies. For example – the well-being check. Recently, there was an older couple out during a storm, because one of them had to visit the doctor. Their son hadn't heard from them, and was concerned. So he called the OnStar number and asked if they would check on his parents. The OnStar operator called them by name and asked if they were okay. She didn't hear any response. She spoke again. Nothing. Finally she said that their son had called because he was concerned about them and just needed to know that they were okay. The mother finally answered. She and her husband had no idea what that voice was in their car, and were too scared to answer it!

So what's next for OnStar? The big news is that now, even non-OnStar equipped cars, can get in on the service. GM just launched a new product called For My Vehicle, that can be used on any new car, regardless of the make. Just promise us one thing. After you become an OnStar subscriber, if you suddenly hear a voice in your car, don't ignore it! Introduce yourself.

For more information about OnStar, go to www.onstar.com.

The Inside Story On... The iPad

For reporter and weather spotter Melissa Jones, there's no such thing as an average storm, especially the last few years. Life in Arkansas has always meant living with tornadoes. Fortunately in her town, they've experienced fewer tornadoes than their Oklahoma neighbors because of the protection of the Ozarks. However in April of 2011, something shifted and spin-up tornadoes began battering her neighborhood. It's a good thing she was able to take her brand new tornado assistant with her into the shelter of her bathtub, to help her keep an eye on the storm and to provide constant communication with her mom – a few neighborhoods away holed up in her own bathtub.

Melissa's assistant? Her iPad.

As a weather spotter for her local CBS affiliate, KFSM, Melissa usually takes pictures of the weather, especially lightning, but one night in April was so bad she left her camera in the case for protection. Armed with her computer, iPad and iPhone, Melissa headed into her bathroom for safety. As the tornado neared, she was streaming the live news broadcast on her computer and the live Doppler radar on her iPad, while texting three meteorologists and her mom. She snuck a peak out the window and spotted a lowering wall cloud, then the rotation down on the bottom. Her two cats were in the bathroom with her and wanted nothing of being barricaded until they started feeling the house shake and dove into the tub with her. "It felt like the house had two hands around it shaking it," said Melissa recalling that night. "it shuddered and shuddered and then it stopped."

The iPad gave Melissa something she and her family never had before – up to the second streaming radar and news updates. With the iPad she was able to see, via live radar that the danger had passed and the storms had dissipated. Without live streaming local weather broadcasts, families never knew when a storm was over and ended up staying in bathrooms or basements for hours just to be sure. Now she knows immediately when the storm has passed.

Another difference is the ability to communicate several different ways. "A woman in Joplin who was buried by the tornado in her basement had her cell phone with her and was able to dial out and tell people to come get her. She lived because of her cell phone," said Melissa. "If my house fell down and I was trapped, I would be able to call out with my iPad or iPhone and tell people that I needed help and to come get me." What makes the newer versions of the iPad different than many tablets, is that it can connect to the internet both with Wi-Fi and via a 3G cellular connection. So if the cellphone lines are down, you can still connect via Wi-Fi or vice versa.

The best part about the iPad is that it's smaller than a computer and lighter, but has a bigger screen than an iPhone, helping Melissa follow the progress of the storm. But the thing that made the real difference were Melissa's iPad apps, some of which are the same apps that her friend, meteorologist Garrett Lewis uses at KFSM, for his own storm reports.

She uses a new radar app called RadarScope along with her KFSM weather app and the app from the Weather Channel. The RadarScope is about $10 but for people in areas with a lot of bad storms, it's invaluable.

Even though Melissa takes her computer and iPad into the bathroom with her for safekeeping during storms, she can't just rely on that to keep her documents and photos safe. That why she's started using Apple's Mobile Me on the iCloud to store her computer documents. If she ever loses a document – or needs to restore a damaged computer, all she has to do is go to her Time Capsule, choose a day before the damage was done and Time Capsule will restore her documents back to her computer or iPad just as they were, before the damage happened.

The Time Capsule isn't just for iPads and Macs. iPhone users can also use it to back up the information on their phones including contacts, voice mail and texts, ensuring that a mistakenly deleted message isn't gone forever.

And those are just a few of the apps Melissa and other iPad users can't get enough of. Another friend from Apple pays all of her bills on the iPad, which makes keeping up with finances effortless, especially during an emergency or an evacuation. Another app helps her track her medical care at a local hospital, giving her test results, letting her make appointments and makes her medical history available to her and her doctor if she needs treatment outside of her area.

Another helpful app is Find My iPhone (or iPad). Just install it on your device and if your phone is lost or stolen it will track it with GPS, play a sound so someone will find it, send a voicemail to the phone telling whoever finds it to call you or if stolen, will remotely wipe your data from the phone for safekeeping.

And those are just a few of the 100,000 apps available for the iPad alone – there are more than 400,000 for the iPhone and iPod/Touch.

The Inside Story On... Lowes

2011 wasn't an easy year for Lowes. With the sheer number of tornadoes, floods, hurricanes, blizzards and other regional disasters, customers flocked to Lowes for supplies to prepare their homes before disasters hit and to repair them afterwards. Not easy, when those same disasters, like the tornado that hit Sanford, North Carolina, wiped out an entire store – while the customers and employees were still inside.

The story of the quick thinking of store employees that day was so amazing, that it made the national news. The store itself was flattened, except for a small concrete-lined pocket where employees rushed their stunned customers, praying that it would keep them safe. Thankfully not one person in that store, lost his life. I caught up with Abby Buford of Lowes to learn more about the emergency plans Lowes has in place to keep employees and customers safe during disasters and to help families across America get the supplies they need, to keep their own homes disaster resistant.

How does Lowes meet the needs of customers looking to keep their valuables, keepsakes and homes safe?
Lowe's Emergency Command Center and network of distribution centers allow us to respond to our customers' needs and quickly replenish store shelves with emergency products to help during preparation and recovery. We prepare at least five days out from a storm, and closely monitor it around the clock. Our stores also have essential hurricane products such as flashlights, batteries, NOAA weather radios, etc. conveniently located in the front of our stores so that homeowners can easily assemble a family emergency kit. (In coastal markets, these are in place June 1 – November 1.)

All of our stores are equipped with emergency back-up generators and we can quickly open after a storm or power outage, as soon as it's safe. Due to the dedication, commitment and preparation of Lowe's employees, Lowe's stores in the paths of hurricanes, have been able to open within hours after a storm.

Lowe's also has Storm Recovery Teams ready for activation. Storm Recovery Teams are employees who volunteer to leave the stores where they usually work, to travel to stores in storm ravaged areas. The teams provide additional personnel to serve customers and also provide relief for employees working at stores in areas battered by storms so that they can attend to personal needs at home.

Do you have any tips or seminars for customers on getting organized, or prepared for disasters on your website?
Our website – www.lowes.com/hurricane - has online how-to videos explaining how to operate a generator, board up windows, tarp a roof, chainsaw safety and much more. It's really helpful information for newcomers who haven't been in a hurricane before, as well as those of us who need refresher tips.

How did your employees save everyone's lives in the store when the tornado struck? Do they have emergency procedures in place or was it just by the seat of the pants?
Our store management takes the safety of our customers and employees very seriously, so we have store staff dedicated to monitoring and reporting severe weather situations, when warnings and watches are released by the National Weather Service. All store managers have been trained and prepared to guide employees and customers through emergency situations and natural disasters such as tornadoes, earthquakes, hurricanes and a number of other scenarios.

To further support our stores and ensure customer and employee safety, Lowe's has an Emergency Command Center staffed 365 days a year dedicated to supporting stores before, during and after an emergency situation. The Lowe's Emergency Command Center guides stores through crisis situations and the aftermath/clean-up phase, and also works with our network of distribution centers across the country to ensure our shelves are stocked for customers when they are ready to begin repairing and rebuilding their homes after a disaster.

How are your employees doing personally after the Sanford tornado? Are they getting their lives and families back in order?
We rebuilt the store in Sanford, N.C. in the same location and it was reopened in September 2011. Every employee was offered the opportunity to work in a surrounding store until the store was rebuilt and open. We did have human resource managers on site assisting with human resource needs and Employee Relief Fund applications. We also had two trauma counselors in Sanford from our Life Track program, to meet with employees requiring assistance.

The Lowe's Employee Relief Fund provides support to employees who have suffered a significant financial hardship beyond their control and who demonstrate a related need. Employees who have suffered damage to their homes and property are encouraged to apply for assistance through this fund. The Lowe's Employee Relief Fund, which was created in 1999, has contributed $12 million in assistance to more than 11,000 employees and their families. Lowe's matches each contribution dollar for dollar to make employee donations even more powerful.

Congratulations to Lowes on doing an amazing job of being there for their customers and employees even in incredibly difficult situations!

For more information about Lowes, go to www.lowes.com.

The Inside Story On... Mayflower/United Van Lines

When a tornado strikes a home or an earthquake shakes apart its foundation, the first thing the owners think of is finding a temporary place to stay. Now if you've been creating your evacuation plans along with us in this book, chances are you probably know the location of that temporary place and how you'll get there.

But what about your furniture? If your home is damaged to the point that you can't live in it, chances are it's also too damaged to protect your furniture and your keepsakes. So what do you do with your furniture and your belongings until you're ready to move into your new home?

We'll thankfully, there is a company that's has already figured all of that out.

After the tornado struck Joplin, truck after truck rolled out of Mayflower and United Van Lines affiliate offices, headed to the devastated neighborhoods. Minutes after the caravan arrived, the oversized truck doors opened and movers started rolling empty containers out of them. Containers for each home, ready to hold and secure all of their belongings. The exhausted families, overwhelmed with joy, quickly packed everything up, so that Mayflower could take what was left of their belongings, back to their storage facilities to keep them dry and secure until the homeowners could find a new place to live. That week Mayflower and United Van Lines made sure that the victims of one of the largest tornadoes ever to hit the U.S., had one less thing to worry about.

Although they don't technically have an actual program at the company designed to step in to safeguard disaster victim's belongings, Mayflower has a network of affiliates nationwide that help as much as they can when disaster strikes. The company gives them the ability to help on a case-by-case basis and the results are absolutely life changing. If a family finds themselves needing this type of disaster assistance, after a large scale disaster, they should call the nearest Mayflower or United Van Lines affiliate to see if help is being made available in their area.

But this isn't the first time that Mayflower and its sister company United have quietly stepped in to help their customers. They've built one of the country's foremost programs to help educate people against mover fraud and to help fraud victims. Mover fraud is the practice of less-than-honorable movers quoting one price for the move and then demanding more money on delivery of the furniture, holding it hostage until the family complies.

The program is called Move Rescue. Mayflower has a team of in-house attorneys that can help people with the legalities of getting their furniture back. Once they intervene, they pick up the stranded furniture and return it to the family free of charge.

So how does a family keep themselves from becoming victims of mover fraud? Mayflower recommends that the moment someone starts thinking about moving, that they go to the

Mayflower website and educate themselves on mover fraud. If they decide to go with a Mayflower or United Van Lines mover, customers can go to their website to make sure that the franchisee they're talking to, is actually a franchisee of their company. They can also go and find reputable agents on the site as well. In general, if you don't see the name on their site, don't go with them. The last piece of advice is to have three estimates done on your home before you move, to ensure that the estimates you receive are correct.

It's nice to know that Mayflower and United Van Lines truly do think of everything.

For additional tips and information go to www.mayflower.com.

The Inside Story On… CVS

When you think about a drug store, you probably think about running in to get little things like cold medicine, greeting cards, a pack of pencils and a refill on a prescription. But in an emergency, your neighborhood drug store takes on an entirely new importance, especially if your favorite store and the pharmacist who knows your family and its medical needs so well, is two states away.

Technology has brought the world together in many ways, but none so vital as uniting patients with the medical information and care they need, wherever they happen to be.

Take CVS for instance. One of their goals is to make their customer's lives easier, by having all of the information that they need to keep your family safe and well, no matter where you are in the country. They call it continuity of care. We just call it a really good idea!

Let's say that a family in Florida uses their local CVS to get all of their prescriptions filled. And since they're already there, Mom stops by the store's Minute Clinic to treat her family's flu symptoms or to get the kids camp physicals out of the way. When the family hears that there is a hurricane headed for their city, they grab all of their hurricane supplies, board up the house and head to a relative's home in Virginia. And that's when they remember that they're just about out of a medication that they need. Or maybe a member of the family was slightly injured during the evacuation and needs to see a nurse practitioner. Because they're with CVS, all they have to do is stop by the local CVS, and the pharmacist and the Minute Clinic practitioner have access to all of their past information, online. The pharmacy fills the prescription and the nurse at the clinic is able to treat the injury with the patient's medical history in mind. Simply put, when you have more important things to think about, CVS does the heavy lifting for you.

Based in Rhode Island, the CVS family has been through its share of regional storms and disasters, but 2011 in particular was a tough one for the company. They lost two stores.

In true "family drug store" fashion, CVS put their own difficulties aside and used the opportunity to reach out, not only to those local communities, but to communities across the country that were affected by disasters.

Here are some highlights:
During Hurricane Irene, a CVS/pharmacy in Margaretville, NY was destroyed and a West Lebanon NH location experienced significant damage. During last spring's tornadoes, one of the stores in Tuscaloosa was destroyed. In these cases, CVS set up a temporary pharmacy in the community to continue providing access to prescription medications and delivered pharmacy items directly to patient's homes. In addition, they distributed free water, ice and other supplies to residents of these communities.

CVS Caremark and CVS/pharmacy colleagues in the region collected and donated first aid and personal care supplies valued at approximately $35,000 to local relief efforts in Joplin. Along with a donation of $75,000 to the American Red Cross in support of relief efforts in Alabama for communities impacted by tornadoes.

And before disasters occur, CVS/pharmacy is on the job, ensuring that all necessary steps are taken to prepare for storms ahead of time. Every effort is made to fill prescriptions prior to the storm, move generators into targeted areas and stock stores with hurricane preparedness items such as water, batteries, flashlights and other products to help in an emergency.

Thanks CVS for helping to keep America healthy, no matter what the situation.

For more information about CVS, go to www.cvs.com

The Inside Story On... ADT Pulse

Last spring, a young, newly married couple settled into their new home in Joplin, Missouri. The couple was so excited to start living in the 1920's brick home, the house that they had dreamed of sharing all during their engagement. It was perfect. One Sunday evening, the sky darkened suddenly, as tornado sirens began to sound. The couple had only a few moments, only enough time to grab their dog and a few keepsakes, before scrambling to their basement to take cover. They weren't that worried, because the home was built with layer of cement inside the brick, specifically to protect its occupants from tornadoes. But this tornado was an F4 and in an F4, no house is safe. Once the storm had passed, the couple opened the basement door and was shocked at what they saw. Only one wall of their home was still standing.

Once the dust subsided, they realized that the wall they were staring at, was the wall where their ADT monitoring system, had been installed. They looked at each other. Could the panic button still work? The husband made his way over the rubble to the wall and pressed the button. An ADT operator answered! The operator waited on the line while the couple ran to their neighbors, calling for help. Once he found out what types of injuries and needs they would be dealing with, the operator dispatched assistance. They arrived before any other first responders, with precisely the equipment and medical aid needed to save their neighbor's lives.

Let's face it, when you think of ADT, you probably think of those "protected by" signs outside of Beverly Hills' mansions. But with the advent of ADT Pulse, this 100 year old company has brought the protection of every family into the twenty-first century, creating safety portals designed to meet each family's specific needs, whether basic or complex. Besides the armed security system that monitors and protects homes from fire, carbon monoxide and break-ins, here are just a few things that ADT Pulse can do:

- The ability to look in on and check on your home with video from any place in the world with a smart phone or web.
- The ability to turn on your system and perform tasks remotely via the ADT app.
- Video monitoring to record intruders, check to see if children have arrived home safely or that elderly relatives are up, around and well.
- The ability to unlock and relock a door, whether to let in household help or take in packages from the Post Office or UPS.
- State of the art monitoring and assistance during disasters.
- Panic buttons and help for people at risk.
- A lighting module that can turn on the lights at a specific time, control the thermostat and air conditioning or even things like flip on the slow cooker or the hot tub before subscribers return home.

As Ken Volpp, Manager of Public Relations for ADT Security Services puts it, "Our job is to keep your home safe, while you're out enjoying your life. We help provide peace of mind, while watching out for their home and the things that are most precious to them."

The best thing about ADT Pulse is that it's completely customizable. Whether you simply want to guard against intruders while you're away from home, or if you need help looking after your family, Pulse and it's remote apps can meet your needs. For example, if your child is supposed to be home every day by 3:30, you can set an alert to tell you if the door hasn't opened or to send you a 30 second piece of video so you can make sure your child got into the house safely. Same thing with a relative who might need a little extra assistance. You can set alerts to tell you if the motion detector in your grandparent's home doesn't detect motion by a certain time, so you can call and check on them. There is even a two way voice companion, for people who need a little more reassurance.

Of course we're only scratching the surface, but ADT has pretty much thought of everything their subscribers could ever need. Which brings us back to situations like disasters and emergencies, when your family needs immediate help. The systems have a battery back-up that last for about 24 hours, even if electricity is out, as well as cellular back up in case the family wants more protection or doesn't have a land line. After disasters, ADT dispatches their own business continuity teams, not only to assess and repair damage to subscriber's systems, but to their own facilities, to ensure that their employees are all right and that their systems are up and running.

For more information about ADT, go to www.adt.com

The Inside Story On... QuakeGuardian

All Ed Schmidt wanted was a better wine rack. Having lived in California for years, he knew that the biggest threat to his collection of vintage wine bottles was an earthquake. For months, Ed went from store to store and website to website, only to find partial solutions. Angled shelves or angled rails might help, but in an earthquake, even one as mild as a five or six on the Richter scale, objects like full wine bottles quickly become torpedoes and subjecting his family to that kind of danger was not an option.

While staring at a wine rack with angled rails, Ed and his brother in law had an idea. A bungee cord. Something that would attach to each wine bottle through a ring on its neck, to the rail of the wine rack. If they did it just right, the wine bottles would move only so far out of the angled racks, before being pulled back in by the tether. Question was, would it survive a seven or eight point earthquake?

Months later, Ed put his invention to the test. He strapped a collection of wine bottles into their racks and stood back as the shake test began. First the test simulated a 5.0 earthquake. The bottles stayed put. They cranked it up to a 6.0. Nothing. Then 7.0, then 8.0 and still the wine bottles and Ed's newly named invention, the QuakeGuardian, survived. By the way, if you'd like to see the video of the test, check out http://youtu.be/otO6dyCRNHw.

Ed is no stranger to disaster preparedness, having been through many West Coast disasters. But it was a family situation that drove home the importance of archiving his keepsakes – not just wine. His grandfather used to own the property now owned by the family of the late John Denver. Recently Ed and his cousins went to visit the estate and are going back again, this time with a video camera to preserve photos of the land for future generations of Schmidts. "It's such a beautiful and peaceful place – it just feels like my grandfather," said Ed. "I realized looking at it, how important it is to have memories like these on video along with the rest of our family's stories." That's Ed's next project.

We asked Ed his advice on securing wine racks, bookcases and other kinds of wall-sized furniture, to keep it stable during earthquakes. "Make sure you screw bookcases or wine racks right to the studs in the wall," advised Ed. "Studs are usually about 16 inches apart from each other. Use angle iron metal brackets screwed to the studs, for additional stability."

So what's next for QuakeGuardian and its inventor? With the success of QuakeGuardian, Ed wants to keep helping people with his product as well as any other storage problems they have. As for his customer base, it's growing every day. "Our biggest sale is going to be an 8,000 bottle wine room," says Ed. "And with the Christchurch earthquake, we're even getting orders from New Zealand."

For more information or to purchase QuakeGuardian, go to the "Cool Tools" section in the back of this book or www.getyourstufftogether.com/cooltools.htm.

The Inside Story On… HootSuite

Even though you may never have heard of HootSuite, it's quickly becoming one of the most utilized tools on the internet, to find and communicate with people or stay on top of breaking news before, during and after disasters. HootSuite is a social media web site that lets users send messages to their friends and family on Twitter, Facebook, LinkedIn and MySpace from just one site. It can be used on a PC or Mac or via the HootSuite app on your iPhone, smartphones or tablets.

If you have to get in touch with your family and friends immediately but can't reach them by normal means, HootSuite lets you write one message to everyone at the same time that will reach them whether they are on Twitter, Facebook or LinkedIn. Then, once you've reached them, you can all send messages to each other in real time, keeping you apprised of everyone's locations and status until you're reunited. Since you can also read your own Twitter and Facebook feeds on HootSuite, you can easily use real time info to keep tabs on the disaster, helping you keep your own family safe. We recently touched base with Sandy Pell, Manager of Public and Analyst Relations at HootSuite for the story behind this popular web site's appeal.

How many different social platforms can you use with HootSuite?
The social networks we currently support include: Twitter, Facebook, LinkedIn, WordPress, MySpace, Foursquare, mixi, and Ping.fm. Basic plan also hosts application support for Constant Contact, Digg, Flickr, Get Satisfaction, InboxQ, Orkut, Tumblr, TrendSpottr, and YouTube, and integration support for Facebook Pages. With the free Basic plan you are able to access all the social networks listed above, however you can only register up to five social profiles.

Do you have any testimonials from users who used HootSuite during disasters like Joplin or Japan, to reach their loved ones or to get help?
When the earthquake occurred in Tohoku, Japan in March 2011, followed by the tsunami, Japanese users were able to easily send out messages across all major social networks, including mixi, Facebook, and Twitter, through the HootSuite dashboard. Our HootSuite community leaders in Japan and Joplin also stepped up to help immediately, coordinating, monitoring, and assisting to spread urgent messages to and from people in need.

What are the best ways to use HootSuite to reach people on many social platforms with one message in emergency?
The most powerful function of HootSuite is the platform's ability to reach people across so many different social media platforms all at once, any time of the day. HootSuite has an amazingly simple feature by which users can instantly send as many messages as they want across any or all of the social networks that they've registered onto their HootSuite account. All you need to do is type your message into the compose box, check the platform(s) you want to send your messages to, and hit send.

Did your company learn anything new during recent disasters that you have used to improve the way you serve your customers?
Yes, we definitely did. We learned social web tools are a go-to communication method, bypassing telephone, cell networks, and certainly email and print. We monitored how people on the ground in the affected areas use our tool, and we've added more languages. Whenever we see civic turmoil or natural disasters, we begin tracking usage from those areas to identify trends for future improvements.

Do you or Ryan Holmes have any stories/experiences of your own that you can share?
We were at SXSW in Austin TX, when the earthquake and tsunami hit Japan. It was all over the TV and everyone was completely shocked and horrified. We realized our co-panelists for our "Big in Japan" campaign were travelling from Japan, and couldn't help but worry. The next day when we did our panel, we turned it into a fundraiser and ended up raising a significant amount of money for the Red Cross and other relief efforts.

Do you have any tips for people who find themselves in the midst of an evacuation or natural disaster?
I think being prepared is vitally important. From a business standpoint, contingency planning is a must. You can lose everything you've worked for. In the case of a natural disaster, not being prepared could mean the loss of your life, or the life of your loved ones. HootSuite by itself is a tool that should be utilized in disasters. You can easily monitor, search and compose messages to immediately know what's happening with a disaster. In some cases it's preferred over other traditional search engines because you can see what is happening with hashtags and posts in real-time.

Would HootSuite still be up, running and available in a regional emergency?
If there was a disaster here in Vancouver, HootSuite would still be up and running. We operate on cloud based servers, that are backed up in different locations around the world. Short of an international disaster, affecting the specific areas of our servers, HootSuite should still be fully functional. For example, in Egypt when the sites like Twitter and Facebook were blocked, people could still access HootSuite to send out messages. We were the only social dashboard that remained operational even through the blockage.

For more information about Hootsuite, go to ww.hootsuite.com.

The Inside Story On... Kingston's DataTraveler

In a world that already moves at the speed of light, Kingston Technology always finds a way to stay ahead of the pack. The number one manufacturer of flash drives four years running, Kingston has revolutionized the portable storage industry with a tiny flash drive designed to take all the bumps and nicks that you can dish out, while keeping your data safe and secure.

We recently spoke to public relations pro David Leong and Craig Tilmont, urDrive Business Manager to learn more about Kingston's newest line of flash drives, the Data Traveler. According to David and Craig, the last thing Kingston wanted to do was to create just another flash drive. They wanted to create a new type of storage device that would add value for their customers unmatched by other manufacturers.

Designed to fit on a keychain via a built-in hole, the newest 8 GB USB drive comes equipped with game changing software called urDrive. The first innovation Kingston made was to add a file management system, to the new flash drives, which not only allows you to view and categorize your files, but actually breaks them down by the type of file, which makes looking for something like a photo or a music file, that much easier. And just in case you can't find the file as quickly as you would like, Kingston included Yahoo search, allowing you to search your files by keyword, making file retrieval even easier.

They also added an internet browser which gives customers the ability to use the internet directly from their drive, without having to use a computer-based browser. Why is that important? Two words – safety and convenience. Let's say you're staying with a relative while evacuated from your home. If the uncle you're staying with doesn't have an internet browser on his computer, using the urDrive allows you to surf the internet without it. And not only that, the urDrive browser leaves no detectable trace of browser history on the computer that you're using. That means that in an emergency, if you need to check your bank account or process other sensitive information in a not-so-secure environment – like a computer in a public library – you don't have to worry about leaving any traces of your log-in information on that computer.

And the design modifications don't stop there. One problem Kingston wanted to solve, was the problem customers had when they lost the plastic caps off their flash drives. In many drives the cap is the only thing that keeps the USB connection from becoming damaged, endangering the data customers are trying to protect. The DataTraveler team sought the help of design engineers to create a special cap that never leaves the drive. It just swivels off and on not only protecting the data, but completely eliminating the problem of lost flash drive caps.

The urDrive software also contains an MP3 player, photo and video manager, an online experience app just for kids and social media connections to help users stay in touch with family and friends at home or on the road, making the DataTraveler extremely useful for anyone who finds themselves in the middle of an evacuation or disaster.

Kingston's DataTraveler line of flash drives – especially the models with urDrive – are the perfect solution for people who want to organize, digitize and safeguard the data that is most important to them, whether it's vital documents, treasured photos or music. It's grabbable, it's secure and it fits right on your keychain. Kingston, you've really thought of everything. Well done!

For more information or to purchase Kingston Flash Drives, go to the "Cool Tools" section in the back of this book or www.kingston.com.

Spotlight on... Lisa LaPorta

We recently caught up with Lisa LaPorta, star of the hit HGTV show "Designed To Sell". Lisa has helped thousands of homeowners transform their houses into spaces that are not only beautiful but functional. Many of those spaces, including her own home, are in California, right in the middle of earthquake country, making Lisa the perfect person to give us some practical advice on making our homes disaster friendly.

Hearing Lisa describe her home didn't surprise me a bit. For one thing it's organized, even down to the garage, which is where we began our discussion.

Whether you're preparing for an earthquake or a tornado, making sure your house is disaster ready begins with ensuring that all of the keepsakes and items that you value most are safe and secure. That's why Lisa and her fiancé started the disaster proofing process with their garage. First, they had their entire garage lined with shelves adjusted to fit the size of Lisa's favorite Rubbermaid bins. Knowing that the bins would keep her old photos and papers organized and moisture free, Lisa set out to organize her business documents by topic, as her fiancé sorted their photos by decade. About fifty neatly stacked and labeled bins later, they were well on their way to being disaster ready.

Being disaster ready is nothing new to Lisa. A veteran of more than a few earthquakes including the 6.7 magnitude that struck Northridge, Lisa knows what it's like to be caught unprepared. "For some reason," said Lisa recalling that night, "every time there's an earthquake, I've been home alone." The night the Northridge quake struck, Lisa, back then a UCLA student, had fallen asleep on the couch of her two story apartment. "I did everything you're not supposed to do," said Lisa. When the quake shook her awake, she ran out into the courtyard and started yelling. Then she ran down to the garage – still in her pajamas and bare feet – and got into her car to drive to her mom's house. That is, until she realized that the garage door was lacking one necessary element – electricity. So there's Lisa, stuck in the garage in her pajamas with no idea of what to do next. Of course that night she was in good company. A major earthquake hadn't struck Southern California in years and most people felt exactly the same way – including dozens of celebrities who had just come home from the Golden Globe Awards only to be evacuated out of the Peninsula Hotel in the middle of the night to the safety of the hotel's parking lot. Although Lisa's mother's home suffered earthquake damage, her own apartment came through relatively unscathed.

Those experiences are the reason that Lisa is such an advocate of making every home as safe as it can be. For example, she always tries to make any glass inside a client's home as safe as possible. "I hate to lose the charm of the old glass and the prism effect, but for safety's sake when I find old glass in built-in cabinets, I change it out with tempered glass." Especially in California it's always a matter of balancing the esthetic of design with the safety and protection of the homeowners. She goes one step further by putting fasteners on kitchen and built in cabinet doors to keep them closed and ensures that the cabinets themselves are secured to the wall. Another source of trouble are heavy, breakable items inside cabinets, like crystal and figurines. Even if the items in the cabinets aren't keepsakes, it's still a good practice to have them anchored to the cabinet itself. Unsecured objects in cabinets can quickly become torpedoes that can injure people during an earthquake, or scatter sharp shards of broken glass on the floor, injuring unsuspecting barefooted earthquake victims. That's why Lisa never puts art or mirrors over a bed no matter how much the homeowner wants it.

But balancing design with safety isn't always easy. While designing the home of a Southern California producer, Lisa found herself face to face with a collection of fragile pre-Columbian collectibles. "I had to research ways to mount the collectibles without hurting them. We ended up using Museum Wax to anchor each piece to the floor of the cabinet and securing the cabinet to the wall." For heavier or taller objects you can also use Museum Wax to anchor the object to the back of the cabinet for even more stability.

When making a home disaster ready, one of Lisa's main concerns is keeping the home safe from the one element that does more damage than any other – water. It's a concern that carries over into her own home, which was built five years ago in a city with particularly strict fire regulations. The reason? Her home came equipped with its own sprinkler system. As important as sprinklers are for fire safety, they worry her. What if there were a small, easy to extinguish fire, like a pot boiling over? Would the sprinklers only go on in the kitchen or would every sprinkler in the house go off? "It would be terrible for a fire to be in one location," says Lisa, "only to have everything in the house get waterlogged. Water is as much of a danger to the furniture and keepsakes in a home as fire."

As prepared as she is, Lisa still has her regrets. Like her videos for example. A few years ago she popped a few of her favorite home movies into the VCR only to discover that they no longer worked. Lisa was devastated. She couldn't believe that she hadn't taken the time to transfer her old home videos onto DVD, while she had the chance. Determined never to let that happen again, she boxed up all of her videos, including footage of all of the television shows she has done since 1998 and took them to a video expert who is archiving them all on DVD. That doesn't mean that Lisa isn't keeping the videos that still work. "One of my most treasured objects is an old TV with VCR, which I'll never give up," she says with a laugh.

Being an HGTV celebrity has given Lisa some great opportunities, not only to help families across America transform their homes, but it's also given her the opportunity to give back. She and her "Designed to Sell" co-star Clive Owen have worked with Habitat For Humanity and did a joint appearance in New Orleans after Hurricane Katrina. Whether helping homeowners make their homes safer before a disaster or restore their homes afterwards, Lisa LaPorta is transforming the way we live, one space at a time.

Get Your Stuff Together
Forms and Emergency Action Plans

THE BACKUP PLAN

Financial Information

Section One — Bank Accounts

Bank	Account Number	Branch	Checking/Savings
Website	**User Name/PIN**	**Customer Service**	**Notes**
Bank	Account Number	Branch	Checking/Savings
Website	**User Name/PIN**	**Customer Service**	**Notes**
Bank	Account Number	Branch	Checking/Savings
Website	**User Name/PIN**	**Customer Service**	**Notes**
Bank	Account Number	Branch	Checking/Savings
Website	**User Name/PIN**	**Customer Service**	**Notes**

Section Two — CDs and Investment Accounts

Institution	Account Number	Branch	Investment Type
Broker/Counselor	**Phone**	**Rate/Maturity Date**	**Notes**
Institution	Account Number	Branch	Investment Type
Broker/Counselor	**Phone**	**Rate/Maturity Date**	**Notes**

Section Three — IRA/401K/Retirement Accounts

Institution	Account Number	Branch	Type

Broker/Counselor	Phone	Notes	

Institution	Account Number	Branch	Type

Broker/Counselor	Phone	Notes	

Institution	Account Number	Branch	Type

Broker/Counselor	Phone	Notes	

Section Four — Credit Cards

Company	Account Number	Website	User Name/PIN

Credit Limit	Interest Rate	Customer Service	Notes

Company	Account Number	Website	User Name/PIN

Credit Limit	Interest Rate	Customer Service	Notes

Company	Account Number	Website	User Name/PIN

Credit Limit	Interest Rate	Customer Service	Notes

Section Five — Mortgage Information

First Mortgage

Company	Type	Interest Rate	Amount

Term Length	User Name/PIN	Website	Customer Service

Contact	Payment Address		

Second Mortgage

Company	Type	Interest Rate	Amount
Term Length	User Name/PIN	Website	Customer Service
Contact	Payment Address		

Section Six — Rental Information

If you rent/lease your home, note your landlord's or rental company's information here.

Landlord	Rent	Date Due	End Date of Lease
Landlord Phone	Payment Address		

Section Seven — Student and Other Loans

Company	Type	Interest Rate	Amount
Term Length	User Name/PIN	Website	Customer Service
Company	Type	Interest Rate	Amount
Term Length	User Name/PIN	Website	Customer Service
Company	Type	Interest Rate	Amount
Term Length	User Name/PIN	Website	Customer Service

Section Eight — Insurance

Insurance Company	Member Number	Group/Policy Number	Customer Service
Type	Agent Name	Agent Number	Notes
Insurance Company	Member Number	Group/Policy Number	Customer Service
Type	Agent Name	Agent Number	Notes

Insurance Company	Member Number	Group/Policy Number	Customer Service
Type	Agent Name	Agent Number	Notes
Insurance Company	Member Number	Group/Policy Number	Customer Service
Type	Agent Name	Agent Number	Notes
Insurance Company	Member Number	Group/Policy Number	Customer Service
Type	Agent Name	Agent Number	Notes

Section Nine	Vital Documents

For this section, note the location of and any numbers or information for your vital documents. This includes birth, death, marriage certificates, green card, citizenship papers, passports, the deed to your house, wills, living trusts, any numbers or documents you might need to access in an emergency to prove your identification, citizenship or ownership of property.

Document	Numbers	Location
Contact/Agent	Phone	Notes
Document	Numbers	Location
Contact/Agent	Phone	Notes
Document	Numbers	Location
Contact/Agent	Phone	Notes
Document	Numbers (like citizenship/passport	Location
Contact/Agent	Phone	Notes
Document	Numbers (like citizenship/passport	Location

Contact/Agent	Phone	Notes	

Section Ten — Storage Unit/Safe Deposit Box

Bank or Storage Company	Address	Phone	Unit/Box #
Cost	Contents		Key Location
Bank or Storage Company	Address	Phone	Unit/Box #
Cost	Contents		Key Location

Section Eleven — Income Payments (ie. Social Security or Retirement Benefits)

Source	Type of Benefit	Direct Deposit or Mail	Amount
Website	User Name/PIN	Contact	Customer Service #
Source	Type of Benefit	Direct Deposit or Mail	Amount
Website	User Name/PIN	Contact	Customer Service #

Section Twelve — Memberships/ID Cards

In this section note any memberships you pay for, ie. the gym, professional organizations, book clubs, or other recurring payments

Gym Membership	Location	Member Number	Renewal Date
Other Membership	Location	Member Number	Renewal Date
Other Membership	Type	Member Number	Renewal Date

Section Thirteen — Family Counselors

Attorney	Phone	Address	
Email	Type	Call him/her for this type of information	
Investment Counselor	Phone	Address	

Email		Type		Call him/her for this type of information	
Other Counselor		Phone		Address	
Email		Type		Call him/her for this type of information	
Other Counselor		Phone		Address	
Email		Type		Call him/her for this type of information	

Section Fourteen — Important Passwords

Email Address #1	Log In URL	User Name	Password	Notes
Email Address #2	Log In URL	User Name	Password	Notes
Email Address #3	Log In URL	User Name	Password	Notes
Social Site Account #1	Log In URL	User Name	Password	Notes
Social Site Account #2	Log In URL	User Name	Password	Notes
My Website #1	Log In URL	User Name	Password	Notes
My Website #2	Log In URL	User Name	Password	Fee/Term
File Storage Site	Log In URL	User Name	Password	Fee/Term
Voice Mail #1	Dial In Number	Password	Instructions	
Voice Mail #2	Dial In Number	Password	Instructions	
Website	Log In URL	User Name	Password	What I use it for
Website	Log In URL	User Name	Password	What I use it for

THE BACKUP PLAN

Adult One - Medical

Section One — Adult One Information

First Name	MI	Last Name	M/F	DOB

Religion	Home Phone	Cell Phone	Work Phone	Email Address

Address	City	State	Zip

Height/Weight	Blood Type	RH	Identifying Marks

Section Two — Emergency Contacts

Main Contact:

First Name	Last Name	Relationship	Home Phone	Work Phone	Cell

Best Place to Reach Contact? Any Schedule Considerations? Notes?

Contact Two

First Name	Last Name	Relationship	Home Phone	Work Phone	Cell

Best Place to Reach Contact? Any Schedule Considerations? Notes?

Contact Three

First Name	Last Name	Relationship	Home Phone	Work Phone	Cell

Best Place to Reach Contact? Any Schedule Considerations? Notes?

Work

Employer	Title	Phone	Manager

Address	City	State	Zip

Section Three — Medical Information

Primary Physician	Specialty	Phone	Alt Phone/Email	Hospital
Physician Two	Specialty	Phone	Alt Phone/Email	Hospital
Physician Three	Specialty	Phone	Alt Phone/Email	Hospital

Dentist	Specialty	Phone	Alt Phone/Email	Notes

Dentist Two	Specialty	Phone	Alt Phone/Email	Notes

Optometrist	Glasses/Contacts?	Phone	Alt Phone/Email	Location

Section Four — Prescription, Allergy & Chronic Condition Information

Prescription Information

Prescription Name	Dosage	Frequency	For what condition
Prescription Name	Dosage	Frequency	For what condition
Prescription Name	Dosage	Frequency	For what condition
Prescription Name	Dosage	Frequency	For what condition

Name of Pharmacy	Phone	Pharmacist	Location

Allergy Information

Allergy Type	Severity	Frequency/Last Occurrence/Notes
Allergy Type	Severity	Frequency/Last Occurrence/Notes
Allergy Type	Severity	Frequency/Last Occurrence/Notes

Chronic Conditions

Condition	Severity	Current Treatment/Notes
Condition	Severity	Current Treatment/Notes
Condition	Severity	Current Treatment/Notes

Immunizations

Immunization	Date	Immunization	Date
Immunization	Date	Immunization	Date
Immunization	Date	Immunization	Date

Section Five — Health Insurance

Insurance Company	Member Number	Group/Policy Number	Customer Service

Member Hospital	Agent Name	Agent Number	Notes
Insurance Company	Member Number	Group/Policy Number	Customer Service
Member Hospital	Agent Name	Agent Number	Notes

Section Six — Do You Have A....

Will?	Location	Power of Attorney?	Location
Living Will/Trust?	Location	Other	Location

Section Seven — Important Things To Know

Things I want an emergency physician to know about me

Things I want an emergency physician to know about my medical history

Any other notes, important numbers or wishes that need to be communicated

Section Eight — Recent Medical Procedures and Tests

Procedure 1	Date	Reason for Procedure
Physician	Hospital	Results
Procedure 2	Date	Reason for Procedure
Physician	Hospital	Results
Medical Test 1	Date	Reason for Procedure
Physician	Hospital	Results
Medical Test 2	Date	Reason for Procedure
Physician	Hospital	Results
Medical Test 3	Date	Reason for Procedure
Physician	Hospital	Results

Section Nine — Alternative Medicines and Other Substances Commonly Used

Vitamins or Herbs Taken	Dosage	Frequency/Last Occurrence/Notes

Vitamins or Herbs Taken		Dosage		Frequency/Last Occurrence/Notes	
Vitamins or Herbs Taken		Dosage		Frequency/Last Occurrence/Notes	
Substances or Alcohol Used		Frequency		Substances or Alcohol Used	Frequency
Substances or Alcohol Used		Frequency		Substances or Alcohol Used	Frequency
Substances or Alcohol Used		Frequency		Substances or Alcohol Used	Frequency

Section Ten	Counselors or Other Health Providers		
Counselor 1	Specialty	Phone	Alternate Phone
Counselor 2	Specialty	Phone	Alternate Phone

Child One - Medical

Section One — Child One Information

First Name	MI	Last Name	M/F	DOB

Religion	Home Phone	Cell Phone	Notes

Address	City	State	Zip

Height/Weight	Blood Type	RH	Identifying Marks

Section Two — Emergency Contacts

Parent/Guardian One:

First Name	Last Name	Relationship	Home Phone	Work Phone	Cell Phone

Best Place to Reach Contact? Any Schedule Considerations? Notes?

Parent/Guardian Two:

First Name	Last Name	Relationship	Home Phone	Work Phone	Cell Phone

Best Place to Reach Contact? Any Schedule Considerations? Notes?

Contact Three

First Name	Last Name	Relationship	Home Phone	Work Phone	Cell Phone

Best Place to Reach Contact? Any Schedule Considerations? Notes?

School

School	Phone	Teacher	Grade

Address	City	Notes

Babysitter	Phone	Afterschool Program #	Phone

Section Three — Medical Information

Primary Pediatrician	Specialty	Phone	Alt Phone/Email	Hospital

Physician Two	Specialty	Phone	Alt Phone/Email	Hospital

Dentist	Specialty	Phone	Alt Phone/Email	Notes

Optometrist	Glasses/Contacts?	Phone	Alt Phone/Email	Location

Section Four — Prescription, Allergy & Chronic Condition Information

Prescription Information

Prescription Name	Dosage	Frequency	For what condition
Prescription Name	Dosage	Frequency	For what condition
Prescription Name	Dosage	Frequency	For what condition
Prescription Name	Dosage	Frequency	For what condition

Name of Pharmacy	Phone	Pharmacist	Location

Allergy Information

Allergy Type	Severity	Frequency/Last Occurrence/Notes
Allergy Type	Severity	Frequency/Last Occurrence/Notes
Allergy Type	Severity	Frequency/Last Occurrence/Notes

Chronic Conditions

Condition	Severity	Current Treatment/Notes
Condition	Severity	Current Treatment/Notes

Immunizations

Immunization	Date	Immunization	Date
Immunization	Date	Immunization	Date
Immunization	Date	Immunization	Date

Section Five — Health Insurance

Insurance Company	Member Number	Group/Policy Number	Customer Service

Member Hospital	Agent Name	Agent Number	Notes

Insurance Company	Member Number	Group/Policy Number	Customer Service

Member Hospital	Agent Name	Agent Number	Notes

Section Six — What I want an Emergency Physician to Know About My Child

What you need to know about my Child's Medical History

What you need to know about my Child's Personality

These are my Child's Likes and Dislikes

What Calms Her or Him Down

These are my child's Food Preferences and Bedtime Routines

Anything else I want you to know about my child

Section Seven — Recent Medical Procedures and Tests

Procedure 1	Date	Reason for Procedure
Physician	Hospital	Results
Procedure 2	Date	Reason for Procedure
Physician	Hospital	Results

Medical Test 1		Date		Reason for Procedure	
Physician		Hospital		Results	
Medical Test 2		Date		Reason for Procedure	
Physician		Hospital		Results	
Section Eight		**Alternative Medicines and Other Substances Commonly Used**			
Vitamins or Herbs Taken		Dosage		Frequency/Last Occurrence/Notes	
Vitamins or Herbs Taken		Dosage		Frequency/Last Occurrence/Notes	
Vitamins or Herbs Taken		Dosage		Frequency/Last Occurrence/Notes	
Section Nine		**Counselors or Other Health Providers**			
Counselor 1	Specialty		Phone		Alternate Phone
Counselor 2	Specialty		Phone		Alternate Phone

Family Evacuation & Location Plan

The Family Evacuation & Location Plan is the place for you to detail where you and your family will gather, and where you go if you have to evacuate your home or your area.

The Basics — Who Is Evacuating With You?

The Basics — Who Does What?

If a disaster or emergency occurred during the day while everyone was away from home, would anyone need help getting to the gathering location? Do you have children that need to be picked up or a loved one with special needs who will need physical help getting to the location? If so, detail those plans below, ie: Mary picks up kids, John picks up Grandpa.

Is there anything else that will need to be done by you or by a family member before or during the evacuation?

Section One — Local Gathering Place

If you and your family cannot gather at home after a disaster, but your immediate area is still safe, where will you meet?

Meeting Location (include address, phone and directions)

If this is a person's home, write in the name of person, phone number, and email address

Section One — Local Evacuation Location

If you and your family have to evacuate your home, but your immediate area is still safe, where will you live temporarily until you are allowed to go back home?

Local Evacuation Location (include address, phone and directions)

If this is a person's home, write in the name of person, phone number, and email address

Notes

| Section Two | Out of Area Gathering Place |

If you and your family cannot gather at home or in your immediate area/city after a disaster but your state is still safe, where will you meet?

Meeting Location (include address, phone and directions)

If this is a person's home, write in the name of person, phone number, and email address

| Section Two | Out of Area Evacuation Location |

If you and your family have to evacuate your home and your immediate area/city after a disaster, where will you live temporarily until you are allowed to go back home?

Out of Area Evacuation Location (include address, phone and directions)

If this is a person's home, write in the name of person, phone number, and email address

Notes

| Section Three | Out of State Evacuation Location |

If you and your family have to evacuate your home as well as your state/region, where will you go?

Out of State Evacuation Location (include address, phone and directions)

If this is a person's home, name of person, phone number, and email address

Alternate Location (include address, phone and directions)

If this is a person's home, name of person, phone number, and email address

Notes

Section Four	Transportation

How will we travel to evacuation location one?

How will we travel to evacuation location two?

How will we travel to evacuation location three?

Will you need to have any travel information with you, like maps, frequent flier or hotel membership numbers? If so note all of that information in the space below.

Section Five	Pets

Are there any pets evacuating with you? If yes, please list their names, breed and ages below

Vet # 1 Contact Information

Vet # 2 Contact Information

List the license information for your pets below, as well as the link to a current photo of your pet on your online file site or family web site. (photos are vital for identifying your pet if it were to become separated from the family)

If your pets are staying in a kennel during evacuation, note all of the information about the kennel below.

List any other information about your pet, ie. Immunizations, prescriptions, special instructions or medical information, below.			
Section Six		**Our Family's Vital Life Lines**	
Family's Web Site	Password	Online File Directory	Password
Facebook Site	My Space Site	Twitter Address	Other
Person	Email Address/IM Address	Person	Email Address/IM Address
Person	Email Address/IM Address	Person	Email Address/IM Address
Person	Email Address/IM Address	Person	Email Address/IM Address
Person	Email Address/IM Address	Person	Email Address/IM Address
Person	Phone Number	Person	Phone Number
Person	Phone Number	Person	Phone Number

Evacuation Checklist

On your Evacuation Checklist, list the items that you will be taking with you, the current location of the item and the name of the person responsible for gathering this item if you suddenly have to evacuate. In the first section, list anything you need to do before you leave the house, for instance turn off the gas or lock the door.

Section One — Before I Leave The House I Need To…

TASK	PERSON RESPONSIBLE

Section Two — What Vital Items Do You Need To Take With You?

ITEM	LOCATION	PERSON RESPONSIBLE
Family's Grab and Go Forms	Ready In 10 Notebook	Jane

Get Back To Life Plan

In this exercise you'll create a plan to help you take care of the following areas of your life in case you have to evacuate your home and are unable to live there for an extended period of time.

How will we handle our furniture or clothing needs?

How will we handle our bank accounts, paying our monthly bills and receiving our paychecks? How much emergency cash do we need to have, while traveling?

What are our credit card limits and toll free numbers for emergency increases?

How will we work? Will we work remotely or have to look for new positions? What people or contacts can we call about temporary or permanent jobs?

How will we handle our medical, dental and prescription needs while in the new location? What doctors and dentists can we use while there?

How long can we stay in our evacuation location? If we need to remain evacuated longer, where will we go/stay? Who will our real estate contacts be, if we need to find new permanent or temporary housing?

How are we going to secure the property or vehicles we had to leave behind?

How will we take care of our pets, during the evacuation and until we find new permanent housing?

How will we handle our transportation needs? What contacts will we need to purchase or lease vehicles?

How will we handle our daycare needs? How will we handle getting our children into school if necessary? What schools or contacts will we need, to enroll them in a new school in a temporary or new location?
How will we handle any special needs in our family?
This is how we will handle the following potential problems...

Section Two	Write Out Your Plan As You Would Carry It Out
Write out your plan like this: During our evacuation we will stay in X location. I will be working remotely with my company laptop and our pets will be staying with Aunt Mary, just two blocks away. We will take care of our finances in this way..., so that you see a clear picture of where and how you will live while away from home.	

Section Three	Contacts You'll Need For Long Term Temporary Housing Or To Start Over		
Name	Service	Phone/email	Notes

Quicklist

The Evacuation Quicklist contains any numbers that you might need in an emergency but who didn't make the cut on your vital information or medical forms. For example, the names of people you deal with every day, like good friends or your favorite service people. If you're evacuated, you might have to call your plumber or neighbor before you return, to look for damage to your home or take care of emergency repairs.

Additional Emergency Numbers

Name	Contact Type	Phone	Email	Notes
Name	Contact Type	Phone	Email	Notes
Name	Contact Type	Phone	Email	Notes
Name	Contact Type	Phone	Email	Notes
Name	Contact Type	Phone	Email	Notes
Name	Contact Type	Phone	Email	Notes
Name	Contact Type	Phone	Email	Notes
Name	Contact Type	Phone	Email	Notes
Name	Contact Type	Phone	Email	Notes
Name	Contact Type	Phone	Email	Notes
Name	Contact Type	Phone	Email	Notes
Name	Contact Type	Phone	Email	Notes
Name	Contact Type	Phone	Email	Notes

Home Inventory

The Home Inventory was created to give you a place to record all of your valuable possessions, information about them, like model and serial numbers, warranty and the location of any additional information. In Step 10 of Ready In 10, you'll photograph those items or do a video tour of your home to show their original condition. If those items are ever lost or damaged, it would help you file an insurance claim. The Inventory is broken down by room and type of item.

Section One — Living Room

Item	Manufacturer	Model	Serial Number
Warranty Number	Expiration Number	Location of Photo/Link to Video Tour/Notes	
Item	Manufacturer	Model	Serial Number
Warranty Number	Expiration Number	Location of Photo/Link to Video Tour/Notes	
Item	Manufacturer	Model	Serial Number
Warranty Number	Expiration Number	Location of Photo/Link to Video Tour/Notes	
Item	Manufacturer	Model	Serial Number
Warranty Number	Expiration Number	Location of Photo/Link to Video Tour/Notes	
Item	Manufacturer	Model	Serial Number
Warranty Number	Expiration Number	Location of Photo/Link to Video Tour/Notes	
Item	Manufacturer	Model	Serial Number
Warranty Number	Expiration Number	Location of Photo/Link to Video Tour/Notes	
Item	Manufacturer	Model	Serial Number
Warranty Number	Expiration Number	Location of Photo/Link to Video Tour/Notes	

Section Two		Family Room/Den		
Item	Manufacturer	Model	Serial Number
Warranty Number	Expiration Number	Location of Photo/Link to Video Tour/Notes	
Item	Manufacturer	Model	Serial Number
Warranty Number	Expiration Number	Location of Photo/Link to Video Tour/Notes	
Item	Manufacturer	Model	Serial Number
Warranty Number	Expiration Number	Location of Photo/Link to Video Tour/Notes	
Item	Manufacturer	Model	Serial Number
Warranty Number	Expiration Number	Location of Photo/Link to Video Tour/Notes	
Item	Manufacturer	Model	Serial Number
Warranty Number	Expiration Number	Location of Photo/Link to Video Tour/Notes	
Item	Manufacturer	Model	Serial Number
Warranty Number	Expiration Number	Location of Photo/Link to Video Tour/Notes	
Item	Manufacturer	Model	Serial Number
Warranty Number	Expiration Number	Location of Photo/Link to Video Tour/Notes	

Section Three		Kitchen		
Item	Manufacturer	Model	Serial Number
Warranty Number	Expiration Number	Location of Photo/Link to Video Tour/Notes	
Item	Manufacturer	Model	Serial Number
Warranty Number	Expiration Number	Location of Photo/Link to Video Tour/Notes	

Item	Manufacturer	Model	Serial Number
Warranty Number	Expiration Number	Location of Photo/Link to Video Tour/Notes	
Item	Manufacturer	Model	Serial Number
Warranty Number	Expiration Number	Location of Photo/Link to Video Tour/Notes	
Item	Manufacturer	Model	Serial Number
Warranty Number	Expiration Number	Location of Photo/Link to Video Tour/Notes	
Item	Manufacturer	Model	Serial Number
Warranty Number	Expiration Number	Location of Photo/Link to Video Tour/Notes	

Section Four		**Master Suite**	
Item	Manufacturer	Model	Serial Number
Warranty Number	Expiration Number	Location of Photo/Link to Video Tour/Notes	
Item	Manufacturer	Model	Serial Number
Warranty Number	Expiration Number	Location of Photo/Link to Video Tour/Notes	
Item	Manufacturer	Model	Serial Number
Warranty Number	Expiration Number	Location of Photo/Link to Video Tour/Notes	
Item	Manufacturer	Model	Serial Number
Warranty Number	Expiration Number	Location of Photo/Link to Video Tour/Notes	
Item	Manufacturer	Model	Serial Number
Warranty Number	Expiration Number	Location of Photo/Link to Video Tour/Notes	
Item	Manufacturer	Model	Serial Number
Warranty Number	Expiration Number	Location of Photo/Link to Video Tour/Notes	

Section Five		Office/Library		
Item	Manufacturer		Model	Serial Number
Warranty Number	Expiration Number		Location of Photo/Link to Video Tour/Notes	
Item	Manufacturer		Model	Serial Number
Warranty Number	Expiration Number		Location of Photo/Link to Video Tour/Notes	
Item	Manufacturer		Model	Serial Number
Warranty Number	Expiration Number		Location of Photo/Link to Video Tour/Notes	
Item	Manufacturer		Model	Serial Number
Warranty Number	Expiration Number		Location of Photo/Link to Video Tour/Notes	
Item	Manufacturer		Model	Serial Number
Warranty Number	Expiration Number		Location of Photo/Link to Video Tour/Notes	
Item	Manufacturer		Model	Serial Number
Warranty Number	Expiration Number		Location of Photo/Link to Video Tour/Notes	
Item	Manufacturer		Model	Serial Number
Warranty Number	Expiration Number		Location of Photo/Link to Video Tour/Notes	
Item	Manufacturer		Model	Serial Number
Warranty Number	Expiration Number		Location of Photo/Link to Video Tour/Notes	
Section Six		Dining Room/Additional Rooms		
Item	Manufacturer		Model	Serial Number
Warranty Number	Expiration Number		Location of Photo/Link to Video Tour/Notes	
Item	Manufacturer		Model	Serial Number

Warranty Number	Expiration Number	Location of Photo/Link to Video Tour/Notes	
Item	Manufacturer	Model	Serial Number
Warranty Number	Expiration Number	Location of Photo/Link to Video Tour/Notes	
Item	Manufacturer	Model	Serial Number
Warranty Number	Expiration Number	Location of Photo/Link to Video Tour/Notes	
Item	Manufacturer	Model	Serial Number
Warranty Number	Expiration Number	Location of Photo/Link to Video Tour/Notes	
Item	Manufacturer	Model	Serial Number
Warranty Number	Expiration Number	Location of Photo/Link to Video Tour/Notes	
Item	Manufacturer	Model	Serial Number
Warranty Number	Expiration Number	Location of Photo/Link to Video Tour/Notes	

Section Seven		**Property**	
Main Home	Insurer	Address	
Location of Ownership Documents		Location of Photo/Link to Video Tour/Notes	
Second Property	Insurer	Address	
Location of Ownership Documents		Location of Photo/Link to Video Tour/Notes	
Third Property	Insurer	Address	
Location of Ownership Documents		Location of Photo/Link to Video Tour/Notes	
Fourth Property	Insurer	Address	

Location of Ownership Documents		Location of Photo/Link to Video Tour/Notes	

Section Eight — Vehicles

Type of Vehicle	Manufacturer	Model	EIN Number
Value/Purchase Date	Insurer	Mechanic Name/Number	
Location of Registration or Ownership Documents		Location of Photo/Link to Video Tour/Notes	
Type of Vehicle	Manufacturer	Model	EIN Number
Value/Purchase Date	Insurer	Mechanic Name/Number	
Location of Registration or Ownership Documents		Location of Photo/Link to Video Tour/Notes	
Type of Vehicle	Manufacturer	Model	EIN Number
Value/Purchase Date	Insurer	Mechanic Name/Number	
Location of Registration or Ownership Documents		Location of Photo/Link to Video Tour/Notes	
Type of Vehicle	Manufacturer	Model	EIN Number
Value/Purchase Date	Insurer	Mechanic Name/Number	
Location of Registration or Ownership Documents		Location of Photo/Link to Video Tour/Notes	

Section Nine — Jewelry

Item	Manufacturer	Value/Description
Insured By	Contact	Location of Photo/Link to Video Tour/Notes
Item	Manufacturer	Value/Description
Insured By	Contact	Location of Photo/Link to Video Tour/Notes
Item	Manufacturer	Value/Description
Insured By	Contact	Location of Photo/Link to Video Tour/Notes

Item	Manufacturer	Value/Description
Insured By	Contact	Location of Photo/Link to Video Tour/Notes
Item	Manufacturer	Value/Description
Insured By	Contact	Location of Photo/Link to Video Tour/Notes
Item	Manufacturer	Value/Description
Insured By	Contact	Location of Photo/Link to Video Tour/Notes

Section Ten — Other Valuable Objects

Item	Manufacturer	Value/Description
Insured By	Contact	Location of Photo/Link to Video Tour/Notes
Item	Manufacturer	Value/Description
Insured By	Contact	Location of Photo/Link to Video Tour/Notes
Item	Manufacturer	Value/Description
Insured By	Contact	Location of Photo/Link to Video Tour/Notes
Item	Manufacturer	Value/Description
Insured By	Contact	Location of Photo/Link to Video Tour/Notes
Item	Manufacturer	Value/Description
Insured By	Contact	Location of Photo/Link to Video Tour/Notes

My Social Life

Section One

My Social Life

Facebook

Facebook User Name One	URL to use when logging in	Email Address for Account	Password
What I use the account for	Instructions/Notes		
Facebook User Name Two	URL to use when logging in	Email Address for Account	Password
What I use the account for	Instructions/Notes		

Twitter

Twitter User Name One	URL to use when logging in	Email Address for Account	Password
What I use the account for	Instructions/Notes		
Twitter User Name Two	URL to use when logging in	Email Address for Account	Password
What I use the account for	Instructions/Notes		

Google Plus

Google Plus User Name	URL to use when logging in	Email Address for Account	Password
What I use the account for	**Instructions/Notes**		

Linked In

Linked In User Name	URL to use when logging in	Email Address for Account	Password
What I use the account for	**Instructions/Notes**		

YouTube or Other Video Sharing Services

User Name	URL to use when logging in	Email Address for Account	Password
What I use the account for	**Instructions/Notes**		
User Name	URL to use when logging in	Email Address for Account	Password
What I use the account for	**Instructions/Notes**		

Pinterest

Pinterest User Name	URL to use when logging in	Email Address for Account	Password

What I use the account for	Instructions/Notes

Flickr/Picassa or Other Photo Sharing Sites

User Name One	URL to use when logging in	Email Address for Account	Password

What I use the account for	Instructions/Notes

User Name Two	URL to use when logging in	Email Address for Account	Password

What I use the account for	Instructions/Notes

iTunes or Other Music Sharing Sites

User Name One	URL to use when logging in	Email Address for Account	Password

What I use the account for	Instructions/Notes

User Name Two	URL to use when logging in	Email Address for Account	Password

What I use the account for	Instructions/Notes

Blog

Name of Blog	URL to use when logging in	User ID	Password

Email Account Associated	Instructions/Notes		

Cloud or File Storage Sites

User Name One	URL to use when logging in	Email Address for Account	Password

What I Store There	Instructions/Notes		

User Name Two	URL to use when logging in	Email Address for Account	Password

What I Store There	Instructions/Notes		

Kindle, Nook or Other Book Download Sites

User Name One	URL to use when logging in	Email Address for Account	Password

What I use the account for	Instructions/Notes		

User Name Two	URL to use when logging in	Email Address for Account	Password

What I use the account for	Instructions/Notes		

Voice Mail Accounts

For Cell? Home? Work?	Dial In Number	Password	Other Codes

Instructions/Notes

For Cell? Home? Work?	Dial In Number	Password	Other Codes

Instructions/Notes

For Cell? Home? Work?	Dial In Number	Password	Other Codes

Instructions/Notes

Other Social Media

Website	URL to use when logging in	Email Address for Account	Password

What I use the account for	Instructions/Notes

Other Social Media

Website	URL to use when logging in	Email Address for Account	Password

What I use the account for	Instructions/Notes

Other Social Media

Website	URL to use when logging in	Email Address for Account	Password
What I use the account for	**Instructions/Notes**		

Other Social Media

Website	URL to use when logging in	Email Address for Account	Password
What I use the account for	**Instructions/Notes**		

Section Two — My Personal Email Addresses

Email Address One	URL to use when logging in	User ID	Password
What I use the account for	**Instructions/Notes**		

Email Address Two	URL to use when logging in	User ID	Password
What I use the account for	**Instructions/Notes**		

Email Address Three	URL to use when logging in	User ID	Password
What I use the account for	**Instructions/Notes**		

Email Address Four	URL to use when logging in	User ID	Password
What I use the account for	Instructions/Notes		

My Work Email

My Work Email Address 1	URL to use when logging in	User ID	Password
What I use the account for	Instructions/Notes		
My Work Email Address 2	URL to use when logging in	User ID	Password
What I use the account for	Instructions/Notes		

My Work Benefits

My User ID/Password		URL to use when logging in	
Type of Benefits	Name and contact information for HR Representative		
Customer Service	Instructions/Notes (include people who can help some access your benefits information for you, in your absence)		

Section Three — Internet Memberships

In this section note any Internet memberships with recurring fees like Netflix, Hulu, news services or professional organizations.

Website	Type of Membership	URL to use when logging in	User ID
Password	Fee/Term	Member Number	

Website	Type of Membership	URL to use when logging in	User ID
Password	Fee/Term	Member Number	
Website	Type of Membership	URL to use when logging in	User ID
Password	Fee/Term	Member Number	
Website	Type of Membership	URL to use when logging in	User ID
Password	Fee/Term	Member Number	
Website	Type of Membership	URL to use when logging in	User ID
Password	Fee/Term	Member Number	
Website	Type of Membership	URL to use when logging in	User ID
Password	Fee/Term	Member Number	

Section Four	Other Websites I Frequently Use	
Website		URL to use when logging in
User ID		Password
Website		URL to use when logging in
User ID		Password
Website		URL to use when logging in
User ID		Password

Website	URL to use when logging in
User ID	Password
Website	URL to use when logging in
User ID	Password

My Social Media Will

Here Are My Wishes for Maintaining My Facebook Account If I Become Incapacitated

Here Are My Wishes for Maintaining My Facebook Account After My Death

Here Are My Wishes for Maintaining My Twitter Account If I Become Incapacitated

Here Are My Wishes for Maintaining My Twitter Account After My Death

Here Are My Wishes for Maintaining My YouTube or Video Accounts If I Become Incapacitated

Here Are My Wishes for Maintaining My YouTube or Video Accounts After My Death

Here Are My Wishes for Maintaining My Blog If I Become Incapacitated

Here Are My Wishes for Maintaining My Blog After My Death

Here Are My Wishes for Maintaining My Online File Storage If I Become Incapacitated

Here Are My Wishes for Maintaining My Online File Storage After My Death

Here Are My Wishes for Maintaining My _____ Account If I Become Incapacitated

Here Are My Wishes for Maintaining My _____ Account After My Death

Here Are My Wishes for Maintaining My _____ Account If I Become Incapacitated

Here Are My Wishes for Maintaining My _____ Account After My Death

Here Are My Wishes for Maintaining My _____ Account If I Become Incapacitated

Here Are My Wishes for Maintaining My _____ Account After My Death

Here Are My Wishes for Maintaining My _____ Account If I Become Incapacitated

Here Are My Wishes for Maintaining My _____ Account After My Death

Family Emergency Plan

(Top portion, upside-down)
Notes:
Alternate Meeting Place:
IM/Twitter:
Out of Town Contact:
Contact Name/#
Meeting Place:

< FOLD HERE >

BACKUP PLAN — Grab it and Go Emergency Card

| Name: |
| Birth Yr/Blood Type: |
| Physician: |
| Contact: |
| Contact: |
| Allergies: |
| See ICE info in: My Cell phone |

Family Emergency Plan

(Top portion, upside-down)
Notes:
Alternate Meeting Place:
IM/Twitter:
Out of Town Contact:
Contact Name/#
Meeting Place:

BACKUP PLAN — Grab it and Go Emergency Card

| Name: |
| Birth Yr/Blood Type: |
| Physician: |
| Contact: |
| Contact: |
| Allergies: |
| See ICE info in: My Cell phone |

Family Emergency Plan

(Top portion, upside-down)
Notes:
Alternate Meeting Place:
IM/Twitter:
Out of Town Contact:
Contact Name/#
Meeting Place:

< FOLD HERE >

BACKUP PLAN — Grab it and Go Emergency Card

| Name: |
| Birth Yr/Blood Type: |
| Physician: |
| Contact: |
| Contact: |
| Allergies: |
| See ICE info in: My Cell phone |

Family Emergency Plan

(Top portion, upside-down)
Notes:
Alternate Meeting Place:
IM/Twitter:
Out of Town Contact:
Contact Name/#
Meeting Place:

BACKUP PLAN — Grab it and Go Emergency Card

| Name: |
| Birth Yr/Blood Type: |
| Physician: |
| Contact: |
| Contact: |
| Allergies: |
| See ICE info in: My Cell phone |

Come visit The Organized Blog for quick and easy ways to safeguard your home, your keepsakes and the people you love, from life's little and not so little emergencies.

Go to: http://rnn10.wordpress.com

Want To Follow The Backup Plan?

Go to: https://rnn10.wordpress.com/media-resources/

For Other Books By Janet Greenwald & Laura Greenwald, Including:

Get Your Stuff Together
Take This Book To Your Parent's House
Don't Lose All Your Stuff At College
Notify In 7
& The Wealth of Tulips

Go to: www.getyourstufftogether.com

Customization and Bulk Discounts Available

About The Authors

Janet and Laura are one of the only mother/daughter writing teams in the entertainment industry. They began their careers in production on network sitcoms at MGM and Warner Bros and are currently developing their own original movies and television series through their production company Lion And The Rock Entertainment.

The Greenwalds were introduced to emergency preparedness the hard way, when a jumbo-jet crashed across the street from their home. But it was a horrendous medical tragedy – one that took the life of their mother/grandmother, Elaine Sullivan – that propelled them into new territory.

When Elaine's hospital failed to notify Jan and Laura of her hospitalization they were not only prevented from being at her side, but they were also kept from preventing the drug interaction that took Elaine's life.

After uncovering a loophole in the laws which regulate the notification of the next of kin of hospital patients, Laura & Jan joined forces with legislators in Illinois and California to enact three Next of Kin Laws, before creating Notify In 7, a training program that provides hospital professionals with the skills they need to notify and reunite trauma victims with their loved ones, quickly and easily, as well as the upcoming Call My Family App. Hoping to keep other families from experiencing the same thing they had, they turned their story into a screenplay called Without Consent, now in development as a feature film.

Get Your Stuff Together gives readers quick and easy steps they can take to keep everything that's important to them organized, safe, sound and accessible. Each section – over 30 in all – covers a different area from backing up and fixing family photos, home movies and music, to creating an evacuation plan, securing vital documents, medical information, financial information and data.

Between their books, blog and website, over 600,000 people have used Jan and Laura's shortcut sheets, action plans and materials to keep themselves, their homes, their families and the things that they love, safe and secure.

Made in the USA
Middletown, DE
03 December 2018